To —

Arlene Lacey

Richard C. Lee
Matt 6:33

Dear Arlene,
Happy Birthday
and May God Bless
You
Love
Ron

Issues
of the
HEART

Issues
of the
HEART

RICHARD LEE

WORD PUBLISHING
Dallas·London·Vancouver·Melbourne

ISSUES OF THE HEART

Unless otherwise indicated, Scripture quotations used in this book are
from The King James Version of the Bible. Other Bible versions used
include:

    The Living Bible (TLB), copyright 1971 by Tyndale House
      Publishers, Wheaton, IL.
    The New Testament in Modern English (PHILLIPS) by J. B. Phillips,
      published by The Macmillan Company, © 1958, 1960, 1972 by
      J. B. Phillips.

Library of Congress Cataloging-in-Publication Data:

Lee, Richard, 1946–
    Issues of the heart / Richard Lee.
        p.   cm.
    ISBN 0-8499-0729-2
    1. Christian life—1960– I. Title.
  BV4501.2.L4252 1990
  248.4—dc20   90–36507
                                   CIP

Printed in the United States of America

0 1 2 3 4 9 AGF 9 8 7 6 5 4 3 2 1

To my son,

CHRISTOPHER JASON LEE

and
To my daughter,

TONYA ELIZABETH LEE

Both who are the joy of
their father's heart.

Contents

Preface

"Be careful with your heart," a wise friend once told me, "for more than likely you will do what your heart tells you."

This was good advice then, and still is today. The Bible says it like this, "Keep thy heart with all diligence; for out of it are the issues of life" (Proverbs 4:23). To try to describe the spiritual and emotional heart of man is too vast for us to attempt, yet each of us knows what we mean when we talk about our innermost heart. It is there, in the heart, that both love and hate, joy and sorrow, choices right and wrong co-exist. No wonder the writer of Proverbs tells us, "Out of the heart are the issues of life." That is why I have written this book—to deal with these issues of the heart that we all face in our everyday lives.

For their continued help, I would like to thank the people at Word, Inc., who are publishing this, my third book. Especially, Beverly Phillips, my editor there. Also, my secretary, Emily Boothe, whose faithful work makes much of what I do possible.

It is my prayer that out of this volume some question might be answered, some hurt might be healed, some joy might be experienced that will lead you to a more abundant life with Christ.

Richard G. Lee

Part One

ANSWERS FOR SEARCHING HEARTS

---

*And ye shall seek me, and
find me, when ye shall search
for me with all your heart.*

JEREMIAH 29:13

1

Who Is
Jesus Christ?

No one has ever influenced this world or its history like
Jesus Christ. He was the most unique person ever to
walk upon the face of the earth. He is the subject of the
best-selling book that has ever been on the market. His
followers number in the untold millions. In the past two
thousand years, people have not only lived by His principles, but many have died for their faith in Him.

Today there are innumerable people who call themselves Christians. Both in America and around the
world, there are countless millions who call upon His
name. One cannot live in today's world without asking
the searching questions: *Who is Jesus Christ? Is He really*

3

God? Could He actually do the things He claimed? Was He literally the embodiment of God's truth? Is He the only way to heaven?

These are questions for searching hearts. They are honest questions that deserve honest and straightforward answers. They are questions with which mankind has struggled for the past two millennia. The answers to these questions affect every single one of us. For if Jesus was not who He claimed to be, He was either terribly deceived or He was the greatest deceiver who ever lived.

"Does it really matter?" you may ask.

Yes, very much! If He is really the Son of God, the Savior of mankind and Lord of the universe, He deserves our worship and devotion. But if He is not Lord, He was a liar and one need not give Him a moment of further consideration. The whole of Christianity rests upon the veracity of Jesus' truth claims. If He was a liar, Jesus of Nazareth pulled off the greatest hoax mankind has ever known. But if He was telling the truth, we dare not dismiss His claims as irrelevant.

I want to challenge you to rethink your entire attitude toward Jesus Christ. If you claim to believe in Him, re-examine the basis of your belief and make sure that you are certain about your relationship to Him. If you are skeptical about the claims of Christ, examine the facts about His life and ask yourself if your skepticism is justified.

There are literally hundreds of aspects of Jesus' life or teaching that one could research in order to answer the question of the legitimacy of Christian beliefs. For the sake of brevity, let me limit our consideration to five crucial areas.

MESSIANIC PROPHECIES

There are over three hundred prophecies in the Old Testament about the coming of Christ. These were written by the prophets of Israel over a period of nearly fifteen hundred years. They date from the time of Moses to the time of the prophet Malachi, who lived four hundred years before the birth of Jesus. They center on the coming of the Hebrew *Messiah* (meaning "anointed one," called *Christ* in the Greek New Testament). They view Him as both coming to suffer for our sins and to reign in glory over the world.

Mathematicians tell us that the chances of one person fulfilling even ten of these prophecies would be one in one quintillion. Yet, Jesus of Nazareth fulfilled them all! While some may attempt to argue that these were circumstantial, or that He deliberately tried to do what appeared to fulfill these prophecies, or that His disciples wrongly attributed these prophecies to their Master, the fact remains that He fulfilled them all. There was no way that He could have contrived the nature or place of His birth, nor who would visit Him, nor what they would say about Him.

Of these three hundred prophecies, consider these:

1. *Born of Seed of Abraham.* Genesis 12:3, "and in thee (Abraham) shall all the families of the earth be blessed."

2. *Descendant of Isaac.* Genesis 17:19, "Sarah thy wife shall bear thee a son indeed; and thou shalt call his name Isaac: and I will establish my covenant with him . . . , and with his seed after him."

3. *Descendant of Jacob.* Numbers 24:17, "there shall come a Star out of Jacob, and a Sceptre shall rise out of Israel."

4. *From the Tribe of Judah.* Genesis 49:10, "the Sceptre shall not depart from Judah, nor a lawgiver from beneath his feet, until Shiloh come."

5. *Born of a Virgin.* Isaiah 7:14, "Behold, a virgin shall conceive, and bear a son, and shall call his name Immanuel" (God with us).

6. *Born in Bethlehem.* Micah 5:2, "But thou, Bethlehem Ephratah, though thou be little among the thousands of Judah, yet out of thee shall he come forth unto me that is to be ruler in Israel."

7. *Of the Line of David.* Jeremiah 23:5, "I will raise unto David a righteous Branch, and a King shall reign and prosper, and shall execute judgment and justice in the earth."

8. *The Son of God.* Psalm 2:7, "The Lord hath said unto me, Thou art my Son, this day have I begotten thee."

9. *His Triumphal Entry.* Zechariah 9:9, "Shout, O daughter of Jerusalem: behold, thy King cometh unto thee: he is just, and having salvation; lowly, and riding upon an ass."

10. *Betrayed for Thirty Pieces of Silver.* Zechariah 11:12, "So they weighed for my price thirty pieces of silver."

11. *Crucified.* Psalm 22:16, "the assembly of the wicked have inclosed me: they pierced my hands and my feet."

12. *Atoning Death.* Isaiah 53:5, "But he was wounded for our transgressions, he was bruised for our iniquities: the chastisement of our peace was upon him; and with his stripes we are healed."

13. *Soldiers Gambled for His Robe.* Psalm 22:18, "They part my garments among them, and cast lots upon my vesture."

14. *Crucified with Thieves, Buried with the Rich.* Isaiah 53:9, "And he made his grave with the wicked, and with the rich in his death."

15. *His Resurrection.* Psalm 16:10, "For thou wilt not leave my soul in hell; neither wilt thou suffer thine Holy One to see corruption."

Could even these fifteen prophecies have been fulfilled just by chance? It is highly unlikely. People usually have little or no control over the circumstances of their birth or death. Yet, Jesus' birth and death fulfilled the prophecies in exact detail.

After His resurrection, Jesus met with the disciples and personally taught them the correlation of these prophecies. "And beginning at Moses and all the prophets, he expounded unto them in all the scriptures the things concerning himself . . . that all things must be fulfilled, which were written in the law of Moses, and in the prophets, and in the psalms concerning me" (Luke 24:27, 44). Thus, to deny these prophecies is to deny the very teaching of Christ about Himself.

CLAIMS OF DIVINE AUTHORITY

No recognized religious leader who has ever lived claimed what Jesus Christ claimed about Himself. Neither Mohammed, Buddha, Confucius, nor Ghandi ever made the incredible claims that Jesus of Nazareth did. Therefore, those claims must be taken seriously and examined thoroughly if we are to resolve our search for the answer to who Jesus Christ is.

1. *He Claimed to Be God.* There can be no doubt that Jesus claimed to be divine. In fact, it was this claim that ultimately led to His crucifixion. In John 10:30, He said, "I and my Father are one." In John 8:58, He claimed to pre-exist Abraham when He said, "Before Abraham was, I am." On several occasions zealous Jews actually sought to kill Him because they could not accept this claim. In John 5:18 we read, "Therefore, the Jews sought the more to kill him, because he not only had broken the sabbath, but said also that God was his Father, making himself equal with God."

2. *He Claimed Divine Power.* Jesus' claim of deity was reinforced by His claim to divine power and authority. In Matthew 28:18, He said, "All power is given unto me in heaven and in earth." It was on the basis of this claim that He sent His disciples to teach and baptize in His name, promising, "I am with you alway, even unto the end of the world" (Matthew 28:20). This command has often been called the Great Commission, and it serves as the divinely appointed mission of the church.

Thus, the very authority of the Church rests upon the power and authority of Christ.

3. *He Claimed to Forgive Sin.* On several occasions, Jesus shocked His listeners by pronouncing the forgiveness of someone's sins. Such was the case of the paralyzed man suffering from palsy (Matthew 9:1–8). Before healing him, Jesus said, "Son, be of good cheer; thy sins be forgiven thee" (v. 2). When certain of the scribes in the audience questioned His authority to do so, Jesus asked them whether it was easier to forgive sins or to heal a paralytic. Before they could even attempt to answer, He said, "That ye may know that the Son of man hath power on earth to forgive sins, (then saith he to the sick of the palsy,) Arise, take up thy bed, and go unto thine house" (v. 6). The power of the miracle confirmed Jesus' divine authority to forgive sin.

4. *He Predicted His Own Resurrection.* Throughout His earthly ministry, Jesus was well aware of His impending death and His eventual resurrection. In John 2:19, referring to the temple of His body, Jesus said, "Destroy this temple, and in three days I will raise it up." On another occasion, He announced that He would be in the earth three days and three nights as Jonah was in the fish three days and three nights (Matthew 12:40). At numerous other times He clearly told His disciples that He would rise from the dead on the third day (cf. Matthew 16:21, 20:19; Mark 8:31; Luke 9:22; John 2:19). This prediction was so well known that the Pharisees requested Pilate to station Roman soldiers at the tomb of Christ to prevent any trickery (see Matthew 27:62–66).

5. *He Claimed to Be the Only Way to Eternal Salvation.* This was the most narrow and distinctive of all Christ's

claims. It separates Christianity from all other religions by emphasizing that Jesus is the only way to heaven. Our Lord stated this Himself on several occasions. In John 10:9, He said, "I am the door: by me if any man enter in, he shall be saved." In John 3:36, Jesus said, "He that believeth on the Son hath everlasting life: and he that believeth not the Son shall not see life; but the wrath of God abideth on him." In perhaps His clearest statement on this issue, Jesus said, "I am the way, the truth, and the life: no man cometh unto the Father, but by me" (John 14:6).

One cannot read the claims of Christ without realizing that either they are true or they are false. Either He was the Son of God who gave His life for our sins or He was the most arrogant person who ever lived. These are not the quiet thoughts of a pious teacher or the ambiguous generalities of a modern day, self-proclaimed soothsayer. These are specific claims based upon precise predictions that only God Himself could perform.

CENTRALITY IN HISTORY

Jesus Christ is the most central figure in human history. Our very calendar is dated B.C. ("Before Christ") and A.D. (*anno Domini*, "in the year of [our] Lord"). In the entire annals of recorded history, there has never been a person like Jesus Christ. He is the most unique person to ever live on this planet. He was not only a great teacher and prophet, but He was the only person ever to die for the sins of the world and rise from the dead.

Napoleon Bonaparte, the emperor of France, said:

"I know men, and I tell you that Jesus Christ is no mere man. Between Him and every other person in the world there is no possible term of comparison. I search history in vain to find somebody similar to Jesus Christ." Napoleon was astounded that millions of people were willing to die for a person who founded a kingdom upon love.

Thomas Jefferson, the third President of the United States said, "Of all the systems of morality, ancient or modern, which have come under my observation, none appeared to me so pure as that of Jesus." The venerable Benjamin Franklin said, "He who introduces into public affairs the principle of primitive Christianity will change the face of the world." Another great patriot and leader of the American Revolution, Patrick Henry put it best when he said, "I wish I could leave with you my most cherished possession, my faith in Christ Jesus. For with Christ you have everything, without Christ you have nothing at all."

While modern secularists have attempted to write Christ out of our history books, they can never eliminate His influence from history. Jesus is the hinge on which the history of this world turns. His first coming marked the fulfillment of Old Testament Messianic expectation and His second coming will mark the fulfillment of New Testament eschatology as well. At His return, it will be obvious that history is indeed His story.

LIFE AND CHARACTER

An examination of the life and character of Jesus Christ confirms the genuineness of His claims to be both the Son of Man and the Son of God. He displayed the wisdom, compassion, and sincerity of the highest personal character. For it is in one's behavior that his character is revealed. What we *do* tells others what we really *are*.

I have heard a lot of outlandish claims in my lifetime. When I turned on the television recently to watch a boxing match, my interest was captured by a young challenger named "Mad Dog" Lee. His name caught my attention. Now, I've known a lot of Lees in my time, but I've never before heard of one called "Mad Dog." So I watched the bout with great interest to see how this fellow Lee would perform.

"Mad Dog" Lee was scheduled to fight the world heavyweight champion. Despite being the underdog, Lee came on television, telling how great he was and how he would knock out the champion by the third round of the fight. I was excited to see how well Lee might do against a world champion. I wondered if his actions could back up his words.

The bell rang for the first round to begin. The fighters danced about for a moment, and suddenly the "champ" decked Lee with a right hand and "Mad Dog" was lying flat on his back. Within thirty-eight seconds, the fight was over. Lee was knocked out cold, and his opponent retained the title. "Mad Dog" Lee made a lot of promises, but he could not deliver when it really counted. His character didn't back up his claims to greatness.

Unlike Mr. Lee, Jesus Christ backed up every claim with a flawless life. He proved to be exactly what He claimed to be. His sinless life was ample testimony to His impeccable character. No one ever lived a life like

Jesus. Even His accusers could not find relevant things of which to accuse Him. Pilate himself said, "I find no fault in him" (John 19:6). Jesus' character was absolutely sinless in every respect. No other man or woman who has ever lived has come close to His faultless character. He never told a lie or broke a promise. In fact, He fulfilled every promise He ever made.

Jesus' character was beyond reproach. His integrity was never doubted. His sincerity was beyond question. You will search the world in vain to find someone else like Jesus Christ. Not one single character from the history of the world could compare with Him.

HIS MIRACLES

No single incident in the life and ministry of Jesus Christ speaks any louder than His many miracles. They attest to His divine nature and power. They range in impact from healing lepers (Matthew 8:2-3), giving sight to the blind (Matthew 9:27-30), causing the lame to walk (Luke 5:18-25), feeding the five thousand (Matthew 14:13-21), casting out demons (Matthew 9:32-33), calming a storm (Mark 4:35-39), and walking on the water (John 6:19). His miracles demonstrated His power over the natural and spiritual realms. Three times He even raised people from the dead (Matthew 9:23-25; Luke 7:11-15; John 11:43-44).

The miracles of Christ were so sudden and complete (e.g., lame man leaping up and walking away) that they cannot be explained away as mere coincidences. Even the skeptics of His own time admitted they had never seen the likes of Him before. Every honest critic who has examined the miracles of Christ has been astounded by the public manner in which they were performed.

But even more powerful and compelling is the evidence of Christ's miraculous power in the lives of those who have put their faith in Him. Two thousand years later individuals are still being transformed by the miraculous grace of God. Their sins are being forgiven; their lives are being changed; their habits are being broken; and their destinations are being rerouted to heaven.

No one has ever risen from the dead, never to die again, except Jesus Christ. After his resurrection, He not only appeared to the twelve disciples, but to over five hundred men at once (1 Corinthians 15:5–6). Every one of His disciples gave his life to verify that the testimony of the resurrection was true.

A PERSONAL CONCLUSION

There is a conclusion that must be drawn from this evidence about Jesus Christ. It is a very personal conclusion that affects every one of us. We must decide if Jesus was merely a man, or if He is the eternal Lord. If He was anything less than He claimed to be, then every Bible ought to be burned. Every voice or musical instrument which sings His praise ought to be silenced. The piano should be muted and the organ unplugged. The choir ought to cast off its robes and go home. Every preacher should resign and every church member quit, never to return again. If Jesus Christ was simply man and nothing more, someone needs to pad-lock the doors of the church. And teach our children that He was the most despicable person who ever lived because He pulled the biggest hoax on humanity in the history of the world.

On the other hand, if our inquiry reveals that He is who He claimed, then we must bow down and wor-ship Him as Lord. If He is the Son of God, every knee should bend and every tongue confess that He is Lord!

I remember reading of the encounter the great liter-ary genius, Lou Wallace, had with the historical facts concerning Christ. Lou had covenanted with an infi-del friend that he would write a book which would destroy what he believed was the myth of Christianity. He would call it *Ben-Hur,* and it would present Jesus Christ as nothing more than the mere man he thought Him to be.

In preparation for the writing, Lou Wallace spent two years in the leading libraries of Europe and North America, seeking out information on the facts con-cerning Christ's claims of divinity and His fulfillment of those claims. But, while reading the historical evi-dence, which in overwhelming preponderance proved Christ was who He said He was, Lou Wallace came face to face with the fact of the living Christ, fell to his knees, and cried out, "My Lord and my God!" He later gave us one of the greatest Christian novels of all time, *Ben-Hur.*

If our search has led us to this same inescapable conclusion that Jesus is the Savior of the world, we dare not reject His offer of salvation. There is no middle ground here. Christ must be received or re-jected. He must be believed or denied. Hymn writer

Albert B. Simpson put it this way: "What will you do with Jesus? Neutral you cannot be; Some day your heart will be asking, "'What will He do with me?'"

Jesus Himself said, "He that believeth on the Son hath everlasting life: and he that believeth not the Son shall not see life; but the wrath of God abideth on him" (John 3:36). That is a powerful statement that strikes at the deepest issues of the human heart.

Every one of us needs to know that our sins are forgiven and that there is hope beyond this life. We need to know that our eternal destiny has been settled once and for all. If God is speaking to your heart and drawing you to Christ, respond by trusting Him as your personal Savior. Call upon Him in prayer. Ask Him to forgive your sins and cleanse your heart. Trust Him to do it, and thank Him by faith for settling the greatest issue of your searching heart.

*Jesus answered and said unto
him, Verily, verily, I say unto thee,
Except a man be born again, he
cannot see the kingdom of God.*

JOHN 3:3

2

What Does It Mean
to Be Born Again?

Jesus' ministry had begun to attract considerable attention. All of Judea was curious about the rabbi from
Nazareth. Even some of the Jewish leaders wondered if
He might not be a true prophet of God. One of those
leaders, Nicodemus, came to Him one evening to in-
quire further about His ministry. The Bible describes
him as a Pharisee and a "ruler of the Jews." This would
imply that Nicodemus was a member of a strict religious order, known for its devotion to the Law and that
he was a member of the Sanhedrin, the religious ruling
body of Israel.

Upon his arrival, Nicodemus began to compliment

17

Christ and to assure Him that he believed that He was a teacher sent by God whose miracles were undeniably true. Rather than engage the religious leader in a polite discussion, our Lord simply looked at him and told him that he must be born again in order to have any hope of eternal life. It was a shocking statement to make to a spiritual leader who was probably twice His age.

Somewhat confused by this remark, Nicodemus asked how one could enter into his mother's womb and be born a second time. To clarify Himself, Jesus explained that He was speaking of a spiritual birth by which one would be born of the Spirit. Thus, Jesus distinguished between physical and spiritual birth (one "of water," and the other "of the Spirit").

As He did so many times in Scripture, Jesus did not merely answer the question on Nicodemus's lips, but He spoke to the issue of his heart. Our Lord knew that this religious leader had come for more than a theological dialogue. Indeed, he had risked his very reputation to seek out the controversial prophet. Surely his heart ached to know if He was the Messiah of Israel.

Some commentators have questioned Nicodemus's coming to Jesus at night as though he were afraid or even ashamed to be seen with Him. I believe he came that very night because he was desperate to know the truth. Jesus had probably been preaching most of the day, and the evening was the first private opportunity Nicodemus had in which to approach Him. Perhaps the Pharisee had heard Jesus preach that very day. Now, compelled by an insatiable desire to know the truth, he abandons himself to searching out the prophet personally. The issue burning in Nicodemus's heart was the desire to know if Jesus really was who He claimed to be.

A PERSONAL RELATIONSHIP

Initially, the Jewish leader said, "We know that thou art a teacher come from God" (John 3:2). The use of the collective *we* has always caught my attention in this story. In essence, Nicodemus was attempting to speak collectively for a group of Pharisees who believed that Jesus' ministry was "from God." Yet, in His response, our Lord did not tell Nicodemus to go back and tell his friends that *they* must be born again. Rather, Jesus very pointedly looked at Nicodemus and announced that *he* must be born again.

Jesus' statement astounded the ears of the Jewish leader. After all, Nicodemus was a good man. He loved and kept the Law of God. He even had a heart for the truth of God that he had heard Jesus preach, but despite all this, he did not have the necessary personal relationship with God. In many ways, Nicodemus is typical of church-going people today who politely go through the motions of religion but spiritually haven't even reached first base in a personal relationship with God.

In his book *Revival at Midnight,* Dr. Angel Martinez tells the story of the day in 1924 when New York and Washington played in the World Series. The teams were evenly matched, and it made for a wonderful Series. Students of the game say that it was one of the most exciting events of baseball history.

They played seven games, and each game was a masterpiece, a pitchers' duel. New York won three games, and Washington won three games. Then came the deciding game, the rubber game, as they call it in baseball. Whoever won this game would win the Series for 1924.

The closing game was played in Washington. The fans packed the ball park for the crucial event, and as the teams went into the last inning, the score was tied at two and two.

New York came up to bat in the first of the ninth. The New York fans began to scream for a rally, but the team was retired in order, three up and three down.

Then Washington came to bat, and the home folks began to clap and plead for one lone run that would untie the game and win the Series. The first two men went out in order, and it looked as if the game would go into extra innings. A batter by the name of Goose Goslin came up to the plate. Two strikes were called against him, and then two balls. The crowd was watching every pitch; on the fifth pitch, Goslin stepped into the ball and slammed it to left center field; the crowd became delirious; it seemed as though it might go over the fence.

The fielders ran toward the fence to retrieve the ball in case it fell inside the park. With a resounding thud, it hit six inches below the clearing point and fell in the field of play. The crowd settled down while the runner was slowing to stop at third for a triple. But the crowd was in for a second thrill. The third base coach, sensing that this might be their best opportunity, signaled to Goslin to try to stretch a triple into a home run. The shortstop received the throw, and spinning around, he shot the ball to the anxious catcher who squatted over the plate.

It all happened in a split second: The catcher caught the perfect peg from short, and a cloud of dust arose as the runner slid, seemingly a split second ahead of the ball. But when the dust cleared from home plate, the umpire with extended right hand, shouted, "You're out!" The crowd was furious; managers and players jumped out to dispute with the umpire on the close decision. It seemed that Goslin was safe. Then the umpire behind the plate told the crowd that he would consult with the umpires on the bases. The fans thought that they would change his decision. The four men in black conferred for a minute or so—it seemed like an hour—while the silence of death seized the milling throng who were sure the decision would be reversed and then Washington would be the winner.

Finally, the umpire walked up to the announcer and gave him the decision. The announcer lifted the microphone to his lips, and the vast audience heard him say, "Ladies and gentlemen, the man at home is out because he didn't touch first base!"

Perhaps you were brought up in a Christian family and have attended church since childhood. Perhaps you find yourself depending on your church or your family to get you to heaven, but you yourself have never had a personal encounter with Jesus Christ. You see, if that is true, you've never touched first base with God. It is very easy to get caught up in Christianity without knowing Christ. It is even possible to live an outwardly moral and upright life without acknowledging your need for a Savior.

One of the most striking truths each of us must face is that salvation is a personal decision. Your father cannot save you. Your mother cannot save you. Your neighbor cannot save you. Your friends cannot save you. Even your denomination cannot save you. Only a personal, born-again relationship to Christ can save you. Only when you come face to face with Him by faith can you know for sure that you are truly saved.

It is not enough to know that Jesus died for the sins of the world by suffering in our place. You need to know in your heart that He died in *your* place, paid for *your* sins, and that He has forgiven *you* and given *you* new life—everlasting life.

A DEFINITE RESPONSE

The new birth brings us into a personal relationship with Jesus Christ. It results from the Spirit of God being born within our hearts in a process theologians call *regeneration*. In many ways that spiritual birth is like our physical birth. Both happen literally and at a specific point in time. If someone were to ask you when you were born, you would naturally refer to your birthday: time, place, and date. Yet when people are asked when they were born again, they often vaguely reply, "Oh, I've always believed in God."

Spiritual birth occurs at a specific time and place in our lives. It is not a process we gradually emerge into by a kind of osmosis. It is an instantaneous birth that occurs at the specific moment that we respond to God's offer of salvation by placing our faith in the person of Jesus Christ.

When a baby is born, there is ample evidence of new life. The attending physician records the details on the birth certificate: year, month, day, and hour of birth. The certificate verifies the details of the birth. But the ultimate proof is in the fact that a new person exists for all to see. Despite the fact that one's very existence ought to be ample testimony of his birth, we still need the birth certificate to verify the specifics.

The new birth must also be verified. There must be a specific moment when you confess your sins, trust the atoning blood of Christ to wash them away, and you are born into the family of God. But, ironically, when I ask people, "When did you become a Christian?" they often reply, "I've always been a Christian." I feel like asking, "When were you born?" Or, "Were you always born?"

Being born again is a spiritual birth that brings new life into the souls of men and women at a specific point in time. Once you have been born again, you ought to be able to point back to that experience as clearly as you remember any other major event in your life.

I can still remember as a child my first day in school, even though I didn't want to go. I can recall my mother virtually pushing me out the door to get me to go to school.

"But I want to stay with you," I protested.

"I'm sorry, son," she replied, "but you have to go to school."

She put me into the car, drove me to the school, pulled me out of the car, and took me into the building to my classroom. I didn't like it, but I sure do remember it.

I also remember graduating from high school, college and seminary, and meeting my wife-to-be for the first time. Those kinds of experiences are not easily forgotten. They leave indelible impressions on our minds.

I remember the day I gave my life to Jesus Christ. I was only a small boy. My father preached the sermon and gave a gospel invitation to people to be born again by placing their faith in Jesus Christ. I left my seat, marched down the aisle, and knelt at an old wooden altar where I gave my life to Christ. It was a life-changing moment that I shall never forget. It happened to me at a specific time and in a specific place when I made a definite response to Christ's personal invitation to my heart.

A PERMANENT RESULT

Physical birth is temporal, but spiritual birth is eternal. Jesus Himself promised that whoever believed in Him would "not perish, but have everlasting life" (John 3:16). Once we are born of the Spirit, we have a quality of life that endures forever. Nowhere does the Bible teach that we must be born again and again. Nor does it teach that we may lose our salvation after being born again. Just as physically, you can't go back to the hospital and get unborn.

There may be those people who profess Christ, but who have never really been born again. They may eventually turn against everything they claimed to believe because they never really believed it in the first place. There may also be times of failure in the

lives of truly born-again people. But if they are genuinely saved, they will not continue in sin without
chastisement.

Those who profess faith in Christ but continue
to live in sinful rebellion against Him prove by their
rebellion that they have never submitted to Him.
Their deliberate resistance to spiritual conviction only
serves to indicate the hardness of their hearts. On the
other hand, true believers will be corrected by their
heavenly Father until full repentance occurs. Simply
stated—real Christians cannot sin and get away with it
(1 John 3:9).

Our Lord Jesus explained this by using the term
"eternal life." He said that those who believed in
Him would not be condemned but would have eternal
life (John 3:15–17). Eternal means "forever" or "everlasting." Now any quality of life which can be lost is
not eternal. Thus, if one could lose his salvation or
commit spiritual suicide and become spiritually unborn, he could reduce eternal life to temporal life and
turn the promise of Christ into a lie!

A LOVING OFFER

Spiritual birth is like physical birth in that it is given
lovingly. What greater human love has the world
ever seen than that which a mother gives to a newborn child? She sacrifices everything she has to give
the child all the love, attention, and comfort he or
she needs. She endures the discomfort of pregnancy
and the pain of delivery because of her love for that
child.

Jesus did the same thing for us when He demonstrated His love on the cross of Calvary. He was beaten for our sins. He was nailed to the cross for our disobedience. He suffered and died in our place. He let the wrath of God against our sin be poured out upon Him that we might be forgiven and set free from its condemnation.

No one has ever loved you like Jesus loved you. No one has ever gone to such lengths to prove his love for you as Jesus did. No one can give you eternal life like He can give you. No one can change your life like He can change it—no one!

In the 1700s, there lived in England a man by the name of John Newton. As a young man he was drafted into the Royal Navy, but later deserted his post to become the captain of an African slave-trading ship. For years he traded human beings for the British pound. Despicable, and the vilest of the vile was this man named John Newton. And yet, on a stormy night in 1748, as he considered the life of his Christian mother, John Newton had a personal encounter with Jesus Christ in eternal salvation.

Repentant of his past life, humbled by Christ's loving offer, ever joyful in his new birth, John Newton wrote these familiar words of testimony from the heart of a born-again believer:

> Amazing grace! how sweet the sound,
> That saved a wretch like me!
> I once was lost, but now am found,
> Was blind, but now I see.

You see, the new birth is God's loving and gracious opportunity for us to receive a new life in Christ. Even as it was with John Newton, by God's great grace all our sins are washed away and there are no marks against us. The debt has been paid by Him. Our hearts are free, and our lives are made clean forever. Every blunder of the past is forgiven. Every mistake of the present is cleansed, and even every sin of the future is removed by God's loving offer to forgive us, cleanse us, and make us new.

A NEW DESTINATION

The future of the newborn believer is radically changed. Like a baby who has just been born into this world, his whole life is ahead of him. The born-again Christian is adopted into a new family—the family of God. He has a new inheritance—he is a joint heir with Jesus Christ. He has a brand new destination—eternity in heaven.

In describing our new life in Christ, the Apostle Paul said, "Therefore, if any man be in Christ, he is a new creature: old things are passed away; behold, all things are become new" (2 Corinthians 5:17). When a person is born again, everything begins to change for the better. He has a new life with new purpose, meaning, and value. No longer are we left to our own devices, but we are now led by a loving heavenly Father.

Some may suggest that all men are God's children. Certainly that seems a nice thing to think, but in reality, that is not the case. One must be *born* into the family of God. Then, and only then, does God become his heavenly father. On one occasion Jesus told one of the Pharisees that he was of his father, the Devil. So, by the testimony of Christ it is clear that the Devil has his children, too. The Apostle Paul tells us that without Christ we are all by nature "children of wrath" (Ephesians 2:3), meaning the children of evil, but God, who is rich in mercy, extended His love to us that we might receive a *new nature* through a personal experience of salvation in Jesus Christ.

The message of the gospel is that God loved us so much that He sent His Son to die for our sins and to invite us into a new life as part of His born-again family. Jesus clearly invited each of us into that relationship when He said, "Behold, I stand at the door and knock: if any man hear my voice, and open the door, I will come in to him, and sup with him, and he with me" (Revelation 3:20).

A story is told of an event that happened during the reign of King Edward VIII of England. It is said that one day the King had to take a journey through one of the most vile slums of his city.

As he journeyed down the streets, his heart was filled with compassion as he saw the poor and needy on every side of his carriage. He called to his carriage driver to take him to the home of the most despicable man of the city, whoever he might be. The King said, "I want to show this man my favor and to forgive him and give him a portion of my kingdom."

The driver had heard of such a man—a man accused of many crimes and considered by most an outcast. The driver pulled the King's carriage to this man's door. The King stepped out, and knocked on the door. The man inside shouted with a gruff voice, "Go away, whoever you are, and stay away from my door!"

Upon hearing this, the King granted the man's request and went away. This poor soul missed a King and a kingdom, simply because he refused to answer the one knocking at his door!

Jesus may be knocking at your heart's door today. If He is, won't you respond and let Him into your life? He is knocking in love, patiently waiting for you to open to Him. Of all the issues of your heart, none is greater than this, for your eternal destiny hinges upon your response. Won't you say yes to Him today?

3

Why I Am a Christian

What a marvelous truth! It reminds us that we have a reason for optimism in the Christian life. It also reminds us that there is hope for those who trust in Christ. Life is filled with hurts and problems which often leave people searching for answers, desperately seeking to find their way. Chasing after one false promise or another, they end up hopelessly lost and frustrated.

But the Christian is one who has found life's answer in Jesus Christ. He has long since abandoned any effort to find the answers of life within himself. In fact, he has come to the end of self and turned instead to

Christ. He has discarded self-effort for faith in Someone else: the living Son of God. He is now building his life on the solid foundation of God's Word, not upon the shifting sands of human opinion.

A Christian is one who has placed his trust in a personal relationship with Jesus Christ. His hope for eternal life rests upon his faith in the risen Christ as Lord of his life. And through that faith his life is eternally changed.

Perhaps you have wondered what it really means to be a Christian. Maybe you have even asked yourself what difference it really makes.

I can give you personal testimony of the difference Christ can make. I was raised in a pastor's home. Our family was one in which we prayed and read the Bible on a regular basis. We faithfully attended church and lived in conformity to the principles of Scripture, but all of that did not make me a Christian.

There came a time in my life when I realized that I needed a personal Savior to forgive my sins. That Jesus had not only died for the sins of the world, but that He had died specifically for my sins. And that it was my responsibility to respond by faith to what He had done for me. As a young boy, I knelt at the altar in my home church and prayed to receive Jesus Christ as my Savior.

I realized that day that my father's faith couldn't save me. I also realized that walking an aisle, getting baptized, or joining the church could not save me. I had to come to a point of personal faith in Christ myself. I, too, had to be willing to declare my faith in Him and call myself a Christian.

As I have looked back over my life these many years,

I understand that there are several reasons why I am a Christian. Let me share them with you that they might help you better understand what Jesus Christ will do in your own life.

I NEED ANSWERS TO
LIFE'S QUESTIONS

In 1 Peter 3:15 there is reference to being ready to give an answer to all who ask of our hope in Christ. "An answer to what?" you may ask. To the questions of life itself! They are the questions we all ask ourselves in our most pensive moments: Who am I? Why am I here? Where am I going? How am I going to get there? How can I be sure about the future?

At some point in life, virtually every human being asks himself these questions. They are the questions that point to the most important issues of life. They ask if there is any meaning or purpose to our existence. And they question whether anyone really knows the way ahead. They are honest questions. They are important questions. They are questions which deserve real answers.

I have found that Jesus Christ is the answer to life's greatest questions. Christ is the way; without Him people are lost. He is the truth; without Him life is a lie. He is the life; without Him all is hopeless. Christ is the center of our existence; without Him life is meaningless. He is the proof of God's love to mankind; without Him men live in vain. Christ is the vine; without Him life is withered and lifeless. Jesus is the water of life; without Him all men thirst for God. Christ is the Alpha: He is the beginning and all that it entails. Christ is the Omega: He is the end and all that shall culminate into God's great glory. Christ is the first and last and all that is in between. Jesus Christ is the hope of the world, and without Him there is no hope.

When I discovered Christ Jesus, I discovered the who, when, what, where and how of my life. All those questions were answered in Christ Himself. He not only knows the answer, He is the answer. Jesus never said that He knew the answers to life and that He would help us figure them out. He never even told us that He would teach us the answers to life. No, Christ Himself is the answer to all of life's questions.

Philosophers may spend a lifetime searching for the truth. Jesus said, "I am the Truth!" Sociologists may spend years attempting to find a better way to live. Jesus said, "I am the Way!" Psychologists may give their lives to understand the meaning of life and how it should be lived. Jesus said, "I am the Life!" Christ Himself is the embodiment of life's most important issues and the answer to the deepest questions of the human heart.

Whenever I have questioned the essence of my life or its rhyme and reason, I have been driven back to the sure foundation of Christ. Whenever I have been overwhelmed by the storms of life, I have been driven upon the solid rock of Christ. Whenever I have attempted to scale the heights of human reason, I have come to the insurmountable pinnacle of truth in Jesus Christ. He is my life; therefore, He holds the answers to all of life's questions.

I NEED FORGIVENESS FOR
LIFE'S MISTAKES

No matter how hard we try, we all fall short of God's standards for our lives. There is not a person alive who hasn't made some serious mistakes that he wishes he could erase from his life. No matter how good our intentions may be, we often fail to perform to the level of those expectations. Wrong attitudes, harsh words, bitter reactions, and painful responses, all add up to produce a load of guilt that we cannot seem to unload by ourselves.

I wish I could tell you that life can be lived in perfection. I wish I could assure you that you will never be tempted again in this world. I dearly wish that I could emphatically declare that you will never make another mistake as long as you live, but that is just not the way life is. The Bible reminds us, "For all have sinned, and come short of the glory of God" (Romans 3:23).

We are constantly reminded of our fallibility every time we make a mistake. Whether it is a minor glitch or a tragic error, we all need forgiveness for our sins. In fact, we not only need Someone to forgive our mistakes, but we need Someone to remove our guilt and condemnation as well.

During World War II, a chaplain came across a young soldier dying on a battlefield. He took him up gently in his arms and said, "Son, you don't have long to live. Is there anything I can do for you?"

As he was dying, the young man's life flashed before his mind. He recalled the sins of his youth and the many times he had broken his parents' hearts with his rebellious living. He remembered the times he had turned his back on God and denied the voice of conviction in his soul.

As he looked up into the chaplain's face, the soldier sighed, "No, sir, there is nothing you can *do* for me. I need somebody who can *undo* some things for me."

Charles Spurgeon, the famous Baptist pastor of the nineteenth century, said, "Sin is a knot only God can untie." Sometimes our mistakes are such that they leave our lives in a tangled mess. Sin complicates every aspect of life. It will destroy your health, incriminate your behavior, besmirch your character, eliminate your future, and shorten your life!

But despite our failures and mistakes, there is good news for every person. God loves us enough to forgive our sins, to remove our guilt, and to cleanse us from all unrighteousness. There is not a single person whom God will not forgive if he will but repent and seek His forgiveness. God will cleanse, renew, and forgive if he will just ask Him.

I am a Christian because I needed Someone to forgive my sins. I realized that I could not forgive myself or cleanse my own heart until I was sure that God Himself had forgiven me by the cleansing power of the blood of Christ.

I NEED HELP FOR LIFE'S PROBLEMS

Life is a big responsibility. The longer you live it, the bigger it gets. The pressures of family, job, finances, and friends seem to grow greater all the time. I realized a long time ago that I could not face those pressures alone.

I knew that I couldn't win the battle of life by myself. That may sound like an admission of weakness to some, but I have found that human frailty is such that we all face that truth sooner or later. No matter how confident, tough, or secure a person may appear, he will eventually come face to face with his own limitations. And when he does, he had better know where to turn for help.

I knew that I needed to depend on Someone greater than myself. I needed a Friend who was strong enough to pick me up when I fell down and who would care about my needs when no one else seemed to understand. I needed to know that such a Friend was there even when family and friends might desert me. I found that Friend in Jesus Christ.

The Bible tells us that Jesus is a Friend who "sticketh closer than a brother" (Proverbs 18:24). He is a faithful Friend who never fails us in our times of greatest need. Because He is holy, righteous, and infallible, Jesus Christ can love us like no human friend or brother could ever love us. Furthermore, He has pledged to love us with an everlasting love that will not let us go.

Jesus Christ cannot fail us because failure is contrary to His nature. There are some things that even He cannot do. "Wait a minute!" you may object. "I thought God could do anything He wanted to do." That is right; He can do anything He wants to do, but He does not want to contradict His own nature. Therefore, God cannot lie because He is truth. God cannot cheat, steal, or defraud us because those things are contrary to His nature. Since He is holy and righteous, His nature will not allow Him to sin.

God has always been holy. It is not a characteristic which He acquired or developed. Rather holiness is *what* God has been for all eternity. God has always been faithful as well. He has not had to work at being faithful; He has always been faithful. Therefore, I can have the confidence that God will never fail me. He will always do that which is just and right, and I can depend on Him at all times because of the permanence of His character.

God never changes. He is always the same. His love never ceases. His grace never fails. He is all I'll ever need and all I'll ever want. This is my God. He is my sufficiency, my meaning, my purpose, and my very joy in living.

It gives me great comfort to know that I can depend on God. I know that He is holy and that He will always be holy. I know that He is righteous and that He will always be righteous. I also know that I am one of His children and that I will always be His child. I have the absolute assurance that He loves me and will always love me. In fact, He loves me so much that He cannot love me more and He will not love me less throughout eternity.

I NEED COURAGE FOR LIFE'S END

I am a Christian because I want to be ready to die. Don't get me wrong. I am not anxious to die, but I realize that death is inevitable for every person. The Bible reminds us, "It is appointed unto men once to die, but after this the judgment" (Hebrews 9:27). Each one of us will eventually keep that appointment. We are all going to die.

It does not matter how rich or poor you may be, you are going to die. It does not even matter how healthy you might be right now, you are going to die. Fame and popularity cannot keep you from death's door. Wealth and riches cannot bribe death in the final hour of life.

We prepare for everything in life but death. We go to elementary school, high school, and college to get an education so we can get a job, make money, and enjoy life. We plan for the future by saving money and preparing for retirement. We plan for our vacations, our children's graduation, their college education, and even for the details of our daily needs. But if we are not careful, we can rush through life and forget to prepare for the final chapter—death.

If the Death Angel were to knock at your door today, would you be ready to face eternity? I read a tragic story recently about a young teenager who was in a terrible automobile accident because she was drunk while driving. As she lay dying, her mother stood by her bedside and said, "Honey, what can I do?"

The girl looked up at her own mother and said, "I need to know how to die!"

How tragic that this mother had not already taught her daughter to die. No doubt she did not know how to face death herself. You and I not only need to be prepared to face death ourselves, but we need to help our children be prepared as well.

Not long ago, I came across an old newspaper clipping in some family momentos. I had never seen it before. It was about my great-grandfather, Erasmus Lee.

He had been a Confederate soldier in the War Between the States. When he died years later on March 18, 1898, the local North Carolina newspaper carried a story about his life and influence in that little community. One paragraph of that story particularly caught my eye. It read: "While on his deathbed, after having made peace with all men, with children and friends standing by, Erasmus, in a low but distinctive voice, looking up said, 'Is that you, Jesus?' Soon he fell asleep in that blessed sleep of Jesus from which none ever wake to weep."

There is no doubt in my mind that my great-grandfather was prepared to die. Search your heart, and ask yourself, "Am I really ready to die?" If not, you can get ready by making peace with God and receiving Jesus Christ as Lord and Savior of your life. Then, when you come to the end of the road of life, you will be ready to leave behind this mortal body of clay and all the mistakes of life and step into a glorious eternity with Christ.

I NEED HEAVEN IN MY FUTURE

Finally, I am a Christian because I believe in the life hereafter. I want to know for sure that I will go to heaven when I die. And I want to know that my eternal destination is settled before I ever make the journey.

When I chose Jesus Christ as my Savior, I chose heaven as my home. I am on my way, not because I have chosen heaven, but because I have chosen Christ. He is the way that leads to life eternal. He is the key that unlocks heaven's door. Without Him, there can be no real hope of heaven in your future.

The Bible warns us that those who are not headed to heaven are destined to hell. The Scripture warns us that hell is a place of "wailing and gnashing of teeth" (Matthew 13:42). The Bible further describes hell as a place of darkness and torment and as a place of fire and brimstone. Hell is a place of total separation from God. It involves inscrutable pain and suffering that no one can ever soothe. What is more overwhelming is the fact that it lasts forever.

The human mind can hardly fathom or comprehend eternity. How long is it? How do we imagine something that will never end? Someone once described it this way: "Imagine that the entire globe of earth were a solid steel ball. Then imagine that a tiny sparrow flew across the expanse of space once every ten thousand years and brushed the tips of its wings against that steel ball. Imagine that it flew off again, only to return in another ten thousand years. Imagine also that sparrow returning time and time again until the steel ball, the size of the earth, had totally worn away. Then realize that at that point, eternity would only just have begun!"

Eternity is a long time. If the Bible is right, and I believe it is, you are going to spend it either in heaven or in hell. You have a choice to make about your destination, but you need to make it now. You can choose between blessing or torment, between life and death, or between heaven and hell. But you alone must make that choice.

Not long ago I visited a foreign country and had to obtain a passport for my journey. When I finished my visit in that country, I approached a ticket agent to purchase a return ticket home to Atlanta. The agent assured me that a flight was available but that he would have to see my passport first. I showed him the passport, and he sold me the ticket.

When I arrived at the gate to board the airplane, I handed my ticket to the gatekeeper and she said, "I will need to see your passport as well." I showed her my passport. She took the ticket, and I was allowed to board the flight. After twenty-two hours of flying, I finally landed in Atlanta, weary and tired but thrilled to be home.

I got off the plane and headed down the hallway toward the U.S. Customs desk. When I got there, the agent said, "May I see your passport?" It didn't seem to matter that I was in my own hometown and my own country. I couldn't even get into my own country without my passport.

Getting into heaven works the same way. You must have a passport, and that passport is Jesus Christ and the work He did for us upon the Cross. The Bible says, "There is none other name under heaven given among men, whereby we must be saved" (Acts 4:12).

The story is told of several men who had died and were trying to gain access into heaven. The Angel who guarded heaven's gate asked each the same simple question. "Why should I let you into heaven?"

The moralist said, "Because of my clean life and morality."

The angel responded, "Depart from me, ye worker of iniquity."

The humanist said, "Because of my concern for others and charity."

The angel said, "Depart from me, ye worker of iniquity."

The religionist said, "Because of my church membership and religious activity."

The angel said, "Depart from me, ye worker of iniquity."

Finally, a young Christian stepped forward, bowed his head, stretched forth his hands and said, "Nothing in my hands I bring, simply to the Cross I cling."

To which the angel replied, "Open wide the gates, a son has come home."

Jesus Christ and the work He accomplished upon the cross of Calvary provides the answers for my questions, the forgiveness for my mistakes, the help for my problems, the courage for my fears, and my assurance for eternity. That's why I am a Christian.

I beseech you therefore, brethren, by the mercies of God, that ye present your bodies a living sacrifice, holy, acceptable unto God, which is your reasonable service. And be not conformed to this world: but be ye transformed by the renewing of your mind, that ye may prove what is that good, and acceptable, and perfect will of God.

ROMANS 12:1–2

4

How to Know God's Perfect Will

The story is told about an eastern newspaper man who went to visit a town in the old West. As he rode into town on the stagecoach, he noticed that there were targets drawn on the sides of the buildings and hitching posts and that someone had shot the bullseye out of each target. Not a single target missed, and every target had nothing shot out but the bullseye.

"Wow!" he thought to himself. "The man who did this must be the best shot in the West. I'll interview him and get a great story for my paper back East." So he asked around town who this man was who shot out the bullseyes. The townspeople referred him to the town drunk.

"How in the world did you shoot out every bullseye?" he asked the drunk.

"Oh, it wasn't all that hard," said the drunk. "You see, I just shoot first and draw the targets later!"

I'm afraid many people try to live the Christian life very much in the same manner. They do as they are inclined to do in their flesh, and however it turns out, frame it as being the will of God. Quite frankly, this "shoot first" attitude can get people into a lot of trouble—trouble that they need not go through if they would simply take the time to discover God's will in the matters of life first and then act according to that will.

"But," the impatient person will say, "finding God's will for my life is so difficult!" Fortunately, that notion is not true; but unfortunately, many are prone to believe this misconception. They seem to think that finding the will of God is like a game of Hide and Seek. This approach to knowing the will of God makes Him a despot and the seeker desperate.

It only stands to reason that if God has a specific plan for our lives, then He wants us to know that plan. It is not His intention to hide His will from us, but to reveal it clearly to us. The problem is with us, not God. We often become so alienated from His plan that we are far astray of His will for our lives. Somewhere along the way we have decided to make our own plan, and that is where we got off track from His plan. It is not that He won't tell us His plan. The problem is that we are not listening to what He is saying.

The Apostle Paul had not yet been to Rome when he wrote his epistle to the Roman Christians, but he knew intuitively that they, like all believers, would struggle with the question of knowing God's will. Therefore, he clearly explained to them how they could know for sure what God's purpose was for each one of them. He even called it "that good, and acceptable, and perfect will of God" (Romans 12:2).

Paul also explained that there were certain prerequisites to knowing God's will, and he clearly pointed them out. If you and I are going to know that we are living in God's perfect will for our lives, we also must meet those prerequisites individually and personally.

A PERPETUAL SACRIFICE

Paul begins his explanation of the will of God by calling us to a life of perpetual sacrifice. "Present your bodies a living sacrifice," he writes in the imperative tense. In this brief command is found the genius of the Christian life.

God doesn't force His will on anybody. It is your prerogative if you want to miss out on His blessings for your life. He will make His will available to you, but He won't force it upon you. Thus, Paul's appeal begins with the words "I beseech you." The word *beseech* means "to encourage" or "to urge someone to action." His appeal is addressed to "brethren," referring to those who are already in the family of God.

Therefore, our understanding of the will of God must be predicated on the premise that it is something that only true believers can know. It is also clear that we can only know His will when we are willing to submit to it.

The first step in knowing God's will for our lives involves the voluntary presentation of ourselves as a "living sacrifice" upon the altar of total surrender to God. The term *living sacrifice* is indeed unusual for there are no references to such sacrifices in the Old Testament. Whenever a lamb or bullock was to be sacrificed, it was first slain before it was placed upon the fire to be burned up to God.

The word *present* literally means to "yield" (see Romans 6:13). The sacrifice in view, therefore, is a *voluntary sacrifice*. You must decide for yourself if you are willing to make such a surrender of yourself to the sovereign will of God.

The term *living sacrifice* is a paradox. *Living* means that which is alive, whereas a *sacrifice* was something that had been put to death. However, as contradictory as it may sound, the idea of a living sacrifice perfectly explains the relationship we must have to God if we are to know His will for our lives. The Bible tells us we have died with Christ and are also risen with Him as well. Therefore, we are both dead to ourselves and alive to God (see Romans 6:3–13).

Jesus Himself explained this concept when He said, "If any man will come after me, let him deny himself, take up his cross, and follow me. For whosoever will save his life shall lose it: and whosoever shall lose his life for my sake shall find it" (Matthew 16:24–25). To *deny one's self* was a familiar expression in Jesus' day, meaning "put himself to death." To take up the cross meant that you were condemned to die and that you were carrying the means of your own execution. In twentieth-century language, it would be appropriate to say: "Take up your electric chair, and follow me."

Yet, in the divine paradox of becoming a "living sacrifice," we discover a *victorious sacrifice.* Our surrender to God's will becomes the key to life itself. We find ourselves living for Him instead of being caught up in the vain pursuit of our own self-indulgence. Thus, it is in dying to ourselves that we discover the fullness of life in Christ. He becomes our reason for living.

The apostle also reminds us in Romans 12:1 that this act of surrender must be holy and acceptable unto God. Whenever the Old Testament believers came to bring a lamb to the altar of sacrifice, it had to be "without blemish." In other words, the sacrifice itself had to meet the acceptable standards of holy worship. It also had to be given in totality. The penitent sinner could not bring merely a leg, hoof, or part of the lamb to sacrifice. He had to surrender it all to the priest. Thus, it was a *valuable sacrifice* of all that he had to offer.

Imagine attending a wedding ceremony in which the pastor asked the groom, "Will you give yourself solely unto her so long as you both shall live?" Reluctantly, the groom looks at his bride-to-be, drops his head, and says, "I'm just not sure. What am I going to do with Mary, Jane, April, and Donna?" At about that time, the ceremony would probably come to an abrupt halt! When we come to a marriage altar, we come to give our all, totally and without reservation. How can we do less in our devotion to Christ?

All too often Christians take the attitude that they are on their way to heaven so it really doesn't matter how they make their journey here below. We act as though we are telling God we will give Him our time if it is convenient and our money if we can afford it.

In reality, we put ourselves, our interests, and our concerns ahead of His will for our lives.

If you really want to find God's will for your life, surrender your time, talents, hopes, dreams, family, friends, and future to Him. Give Him your job, your hobbies, and your habits. Let go of your own control, and surrender to His control. Give it all to Him, and you will never regret it.

A PERMANENT SEPARATION

Our salvation is described in Scripture as a spiritual marriage to Christ. In a very real sense, we have divorced the world and married Him. Now that the vows have been pledged and the transaction has been completed by faith, we are reminded by the Apostle Paul that we must remain separated from the world in order to be devoted unto Christ.

"Be not conformed to this world" is the admonition of the apostle. The word *conformed* means "to press into the image." It denotes the idea of pressing an object into soft clay until the clay takes on the image of that object. The *Phillip's* translation of Romans 12:2 puts it like this: "Don't let the world squeeze you into its mold." I would put it this way: "Don't let the world pressure you into its lifestyle."

The world is the biblical term for the world system controlled by Satan, whom the Scripture calls "the god of this world" (2 Corinthians 4:4). During this present dispensation, Satan is fully operable in our world. That is why the world is filled with sin, evil, murder, rape, pornography, robbery, and war.

Where he is in control, Satan brings havoc and destruction.

Of the greatest struggles of the Christian life is the battle we all face against the world, the flesh, and the Devil. The temptation is ever present to lure us back into the very lifestyle from which we were delivered. People will even pressure you to give in to temptation so they don't have to feel guilty and alone in their sin. One of the most difficult things about winning people to Christ today is that they usually know too many Christians who don't act like Christians. Unfortunately, unseparated Christians who are still living for the world do more harm to the cause of Christ than unbelievers do to hinder the gospel.

I have often witnessed to someone who has pointed an accusing finger at the failures of a professing Christian and said, "If Christianity changes you so much, why didn't it change my husband . . . wife . . . neighbor . . . relative?" Usually, the person goes on to say something like, "Why should I bother to give my life to Christ if it isn't going to make any real difference in my living?"

If you really want to find God's will for your life, you will only find it in a permanent separation from the world. You cannot continue to live, act, talk, think, and behave like the world and expect God to bless your life. His pattern for successful living not only involves our being saved from the penalty of sin, but being separated from the practice of sin.

Worldly lifestyles and involvements which are debauchery to God have no place in the Christian life. Those things which once held a firm grip upon our lives will attempt to clutch at us again if we allow them access. Learning to live a successful Christian life, therefore, involves staying away from those things that will pull us down in our walk with God.

A POWERFUL TRANSFORMATION

Living the Christian life in the will of God involves a powerful inner transformation of mind and spirit. In Romans 12:2 the Apostle Paul says, "Be ye transformed by the renewing of your mind." Many of us have good intentions, but those intentions never become actions. We want to live in the center of God's will, but we always excuse ourselves by simply saying, "I can't do it." The only reason we can't is because we really don't want to do it.

Whenever our inner attitudes are changed, they will always result in changed actions. The biblical concept of repentance clearly teaches this truth: In the Hebrew Old Testament, the word *repent* (*shub*) means "to turn away" from sin. In the Greek New Testament, the word *repent* (*metanoia*) means a "change of mind." Together, they emphasize the concept that a true change of mind always results in a change in one's direction in life.

When we truly surrender our lives to Christ in an act of sacrifice and separation, we then will be in a place where our minds can be transformed by the Spirit of God. As He begins that transforming work in our minds, the Holy Spirit begins to conform us to the image of Christ. Those things of the flesh which were once so tempting to us begin to become insignificant. Their tantalizing appeal begins to cheapen by contrast to the greatness of God. That which we once valued in the world, we now despise, and that which we once despised, we now value. Our minds have been transformed.

The word *transformed* translates the term *metamorphosis* in the original Greek. It implies a basic change in the Christian's inward nature and results in a brand new pattern of character and behavior that corresponds to our new nature in Christ. It is such a drastic change that it alters our entire being.

Metamorphosis is the term used to describe the transformation of a caterpillar into a butterfly. Have you ever observed a caterpillar crawling along the sidewalk? They aren't a pleasant sight. They are slimy, fuzzy, and squishy, but they eventually spin themselves into cocoons. Even the cocoons aren't pleasant to see. But inside those gray little incubators, an incredible transformation is taking place. Finally, the cocoon will break open, and a beautiful butterfly will emerge with all the striking colors nature can give.

The transformation of a caterpillar into a butterfly is so drastic that it is hard to believe the butterfly was ever a caterpillar. That same incredible process occurs every time a person is transformed into a child of God by the life-changing power of God's grace. The Bible simply states it like this: "Therefore if any man be in Christ, he is a new creature: old things are passed away; behold, all things are become new" (2 Corinthians 5:17).

When you and I come to the end of ourselves, we stop trying to make ourselves better by our own self-effort. Only when we are willing to abandon the philosophies of this world and surrender to the will of God, will we ever find true meaning and happiness in life. When we stop working, God begins to work. When we start trusting, He starts transforming. Spurgeon said it, and it is true, "We cannot always trace God's hand, but we can always trust God's heart."

A PERFECT SOLUTION

When I was a teenager, like many young people, I was almost afraid of the will of God. I seemed to think that if I let God rule my life, something terrible would happen. But as I grew in my walk with the Lord, I came to realize that His will was the perfect plan for my life.

Romans 12:2 also reminds us that when we have been transformed by the power of God, we will begin to experience "that good, and acceptable, and perfect will of God" for our lives. When you give up the things of the world in order to live in the will of God, you will find that He replaces those things that once seemed so important to you with things that are far greater and better.

The things of this life will eventually pass away, but he who does the will of God will abide forever. If you really want to make a lasting contribution to this world, turn loose of it. For when it loses its grip on you, you will see it in its proper perspective. All that the world is or has to offer is temporal and passing away.

Finally, we come to the full realization that only what is done for Christ will stand the test of time. God has forgiven us and brought us into His family so that we might serve Him. He has called us to an act of obedience by which we determine to serve Him at all times.

God never leaves His purposes to guesswork. He clearly tells us in the Bible what He wants us to do. The key to discerning His will is not where we go or what we do so much as it is in becoming what He wants us to be. His principles for life are laid out in the Scriptures which serve as our guide. As we prayerfully seek His guidance, He promises to lead us into each step of life according to His perfect will. We simply must be willing to follow.

> It may not be on the mountain's height,
> Or over the stormy sea;
> It may not be at the battle's front,
> My Lord will have need of me;
>
> But if by a still small voice He calls
> To paths I do not know,
> I'll answer, dear Lord, with my hand in Thine,
> I'll go where you want me to go,
>
> I'll go where you want me to go, dear Lord,
> O'er mountain, or plain, or sea;
> I'll say what you want me to say, dear Lord,
> I'll be what you want me to be.

—Mary Brown

Part Two

HEARTS OF PRAYER

*Whosoever shall say unto this
mountain, Be thou removed . . .
and shall not doubt in his heart, but
shall believe that those things which
he saith shall come to pass; he shall
have whatsoever he saith.*

MARK 11:23

Ask, and it shall be given you; seek, and ye shall find; knock, and it shall be opened unto you. For every one that asketh receiveth; and he that seeketh findeth; and to him that knocketh it shall be opened.

LUKE 11:9–10

5

Praying for Those We Love

Praying for others is called intercessory prayer. It involves our interceding with God on behalf of someone else. It is the kind of praying that parents do for their children and that good friends do for one another. Perhaps you have a friend or loved one for whom you have been praying. Is it working? Is your prayer really making a difference in that person's life?

Jesus had much to say about learning to pray. On several occasions He took time to teach His disciples the principles for getting their prayers answered. That was the context of the passage in Luke 11. The disciples had come to Jesus and asked of Him, "Teach us to

59

pray," and in His response He not only taught them a model prayer (often called the Lord's Prayer), but He also gave an illustration to explain to them how intercessory prayer worked.

The story that Jesus told was that of a man who had a friend to come to his home late one night from a long journey in need of food and shelter. In gracious hospitality, the host took his friend in, but quickly discovered that he was short of food to meet the need of this traveler. So the host went to the next-door neighbor's house in the middle of the night and awakened him, asking that he might borrow three loaves of bread to feed his traveling friend. The neighbor responded, "Trouble me not: the door is now shut, and my children are with me in bed; I cannot rise and give thee" (Luke 11:7).

Now in ancient times, the entire family would often sleep on mats on the floor, all together in one room. For the man to get up and help his neighbor, it might have meant crawling over the children and waking them as well. Thus, he was reluctant to help. But as Jesus continued the story, He said that the host kept banging on the door and asking for help until the neighbor finally got up, came to the door, and filled his request.

At first, this seems only to be the story of a neighbor's persistence in his requesting bread. But we must remember that it was told by our Lord in context with His teachings concerning prayer. Therefore, through careful examination, we should be able to glean from it insightful principles concerning how we are to pray for others. Let's look and see what truths this story holds for us in praying for those whom we love.

ASK FOR ALL YOU NEED

I have always been intrigued by the fact that the man in the illustration asked for *three* loaves of bread at midnight. In those days a loaf of bread was usually sufficient to feed a family for a whole day. Yet, this man asked his neighbor for three whole loaves to feed his friend who probably needed little more than a snack at that hour of the night.

Why such a strange request? Why did he ask for so many loaves? The answer is, because that was what he desired. He asked for *all* that he wanted, and he got it. When we begin to understand who our God is, we will stop asking Him only for the mediocre, and we will begin to ask for the magnificent because our God is not a mediocre God. He is the magnificent and almighty God. He can do exceedingly more than we could ever think to ask.

The Bible says, "Ye have not, because ye ask not" (James 4:2). All too often we go through life like spiritual beggars—content with the crumbs from the Father's table when we could have the abundance of His blessings. Don't be afraid to ask God for all that you need. Don't demand it or ask presumptuously, but don't hesitate to ask Him for all that is on your heart. He is the King of Kings. He owns the cattle on a thousand hills and the wealth in every mine. What is even more wonderful is the fact that He wants to answer your prayers and meet your needs.

God is always honored when we ask Him for large amounts. It is our way of telling Him that we know that He is great enough to meet our needs. Now we can certainly ask Him for the small things as well, but I believe it especially honors Him when we trust Him for greater things.

Imagine that you were the coach of a professional football team with a running back like the famous Walter Payton. It is third down in the closing minutes of the game. Your team is trailing by six points, and you have the ball just ten yards from your opponent's goal line. It would not make much sense to call Walter aside and say, "Just try to get us a half yard, Walter." With a running back like that, you would ask him to try to go all the way for the touchdown. Such a request would be according to his capability.

The same thing is true of our requests of God. If we ask according to His capability to answer, the Scripture promises, "Ye shall ask what ye will, and it shall be done unto you" (John 15:7). The Bible also tells us that God is seeking those to whom He might show Himself strong on their behalf (2 Chronicles 16:9). Think of it—God is looking for people who are willing to believe that He can do all that He promised to do on their behalf.

The most important posture of prayer is that of *faith* which enables us to come boldly before His throne to seek help in time of need. It is not ourselves, our flesh, nor our ability that we trust at such times. It is our faith in His great grace that encourages us to go boldly unto God with our requests. He is a great God, and He is honored with your greatest requests. Don't be afraid to ask, no matter how great your need.

TOTALLY DEPEND ON GOD

Effective prayer also involves our total dependence on God. It results from the realization that all we have is a gift from Him. In our story, the man who went to his neighbor said, "I have nothing to set before him" (Luke 11:6). That was a statement of total dependence. He was pleading with his friend out of complete desperation. He had searched his cupboards and found them bare. His resources were inadequate, and he had to depend on someone else to meet his need.

In reality, we have nothing apart from God. Your house, your land, and your car can all be gone in a moment. Your bank account can collapse and your health can disintegrate overnight. All that we have can vanish in the twinkling of an eye. Over the years of my ministry, I have counseled many a successful business person whose fortune had disappeared and who was driven to the very point of financial disaster by one wrong decision.

Our only real security is in Jesus Christ. He is the only true reality of life. He is our only sufficiency. With that in mind, we must come to Him, praying in total dependence upon Him to meet our needs or the needs of another. But I am afraid that many of us pray only casually, "God, help my son, save my daughter, or meet my needs." Such prayers are muttered in passing as we rush about our busy lives. They are often vain, repetitious words, recited again and again without much thought.

It is not the arithmetic of our prayers that moves God. The number of times we pray may be irrelevant. It is not the rhetoric of our prayers that impresses God. He can see through our words and phrases. It is not the geometry of prayer that reaches heaven. The length of our prayers may not matter at all if they are but endless drones. It is not the music of prayer that is pleasant to the ear or the logic of prayer that impresses the mind which ascends the gates of heaven. It is the *heart* of our praying which moves the heart of God.

God is not impressed with our eloquence, logic, or grammar. He really does not listen to all of that so much as He is attentive to the intentions of the heart. He listens to the heart cry of His children who call upon Him with believing faith and total dependence upon His willingness to answer. It does not matter who you are or from which level of society you come. Whether you are highly educated or whether you cannot read or write does not limit your ability to pray. You can still have power with God because He does not look upon our outward appearance. He looks upon our hearts.

RISK THE CRITICISM OF OTHERS

Prayer is not an easy process. Often we must be willing to risk the criticism of others to move the heart of God. Notice again the man in our story. He was out at midnight asking for help. Everyone was sound asleep when he arrived at his friend's house. I can imagine the dogs began to bark and the neighbors awoke to see who was making all this racket in the middle of the night.

"Doesn't he know what time it is?" they may have asked themselves.

"Be quiet," they might have shouted. "You will wake up my children, too!"

If you have ever had the phone ring in the middle of the night or had someone knocking at the door, you can imagine this scene. It is never pleasant to be aroused from bed to answer the door at such an hour. You can also imagine the reaction of the friend and all who were in his house. Attempting to avoid such chaos, the friend told his neighbor not to bother him and not to awaken his children.

But the man with the need kept on knocking. He did not go away politely or quietly. Instead he kept knocking and calling out all the more persistently. He did not give up regardless of the criticism he received. The Bible calls his insistence "importunity," which translates the Greek word *anaideia*, meaning "shameless persistence." An even stronger translation would be "impudence" or "boldness." Such persistence will always be criticized by others with less faith in God or less confidence in the promises of His Word.

Prayer that moves the heart of God is willing to risk all in order to receive an answer. The man pounding on the door was risking the friendship of his neighbor and the ill will of the entire neighborhood. But he kept on knocking because his need was great.

I have always been amazed at the story recorded in Acts 12 of the early church praying for Peter's release from prison. Peter had been imprisoned for preaching the gospel and was chained between two Roman soldiers. In the meantime, the Christians gathered at the home of Mary, the mother of Mark, to pray for Peter's release. As they began to pray, God sent His angel to set Peter free. The angel took off his shackles and walked him right through the gate and onto the street in the middle of the night.

Excited about his miraculous release from prison, Peter made his way through the empty streets to Mary's house. When he knocked at the gate entrance, the people sent a young girl named Rhoda to answer the door. When she discovered it was Peter, she left him standing there and ran to tell the others. Instead of praising God for their answered prayers, they all began criticizing the girl for making such a ridiculous statement. "Thou art mad," they insisted.

The entire group had been praying for Peter's release, but when the answer came, they refused to believe it. Rhoda finally had to send them all to the gate to see for themselves. If even these believers criticize the one who brought them word of an answered prayer, just think what those of the world will say when someone risks all to receive an answer to prayer. Those of the world cannot imagine risking all for the cause of Christ, so when you do, you will be criticized.

Don't hold back because of the criticism of others. Trust God, and walk by faith. If He said it, that's enough for me to believe it. Trust Him, and move ahead by faith.

SACRIFICE WHATEVER IS NECESSARY

The man who went to his neighbor in desperation had to sacrifice his pride and reputation to get his need met. He may have been an upstanding member of the community, but he was out at midnight begging for bread. He laid his reputation on the line in order to feed his friend. No personal considerations of his own held him back from his pursuit. He sacrificed all that others might have thought to intercede for his friend.

In order to see your prayers answered, you may have to sacrifice time and effort as well. I have had many people ask me to pray for the salvation of a friend, relative, or loved one over the years. When I have asked them whether they have personally talked to that person about Jesus, they usually say, "Oh, I could never do that. I'm too close to him. He won't listen to me."

The real problem is that some have too much fleshly pride to tell others about Christ because we are afraid of criticism or rejection. If you are not willing to sacrifice your pride in order to witness to others, don't expect God to send someone else to them.

I have also noticed over the years that some people will pray for the lost and starving children all over the world, and all the while will not help those in need in their own community. There is nothing wrong with being concerned about the needs of the world, but all too often those needs are intangible, whereas the needs of those in our own city are more real.

It is hypocritical to pray for the needs of those we have never seen when we are unwilling to help those we have seen. It is futile to think we can care about those far away when we are unwilling to reach out to those near at hand. If you are not willing to feed the hungry at home, you will not likely feed them abroad. If you are not willing to help the children in your neighborhood by bringing them to the local church, you will not likely give your time and effort to reach out to the children in a foreign land, no matter how hard you pray for them.

I am convinced that God wants to know whether we really mean business with Him when we pray. Genuine prayer will be backed up by personal sacrifice. When we are willing to do whatever is necessary to serve God is when we can be assured that He will do whatever is necessary to help us.

PRAY UNTIL THE ANSWER COMES

The ultimate lesson in this story is that we must keep on praying and not give up. The man was initially rejected by his neighbor because of the inconvenience of the whole situation. His family was asleep on the floor, and he did not want to awaken them. Nevertheless, he finally arose to get the loaves of bread, not because of their friendship, but because of the man's persistence.

Visualize the scene again. The man is in bed on a mat near the window and the furthest from the door. His wife and children are sound asleep. Everything in the house is peaceful and quiet. Suddenly the knock comes at the door. There is no response. The man continues knocking and starts calling out to his friend. I can imagine the husband sitting up in bed, struggling to wake up and telling the man at the door to be quiet and go away. But because of the man's persistence, he finally arises, lights a candle, stumbles over the children, and makes his way to the kitchen to get the loaves of bread.

Jesus' main message in this story is to teach us not to give up in prayer. No matter how long we have wrestled over a given matter with God, we must not give up until our prayer is answered.

In Genesis 32 we read about Jacob's wrestling with the Angel of the Lord. Jacob had been a rascal and manipulator all his life. Yet, he wrestled with the angel all night and told the angel, "I will not let you go until you bless me" (TLB). Finally, the angel told Jacob that because he had prevailed with God he would henceforth be known as Israel, "A prince with God."

Our Lord put it this way when He said, "Ask, and it shall be given you; seek, and ye shall find; knock, and it shall be opened unto you" (Luke 11:9). In the original Greek, these are present active imperatives. That means they are translated in the present tense: "Ask, and keep on asking; seek, and keep on seeking; knock, and keep on knocking."

If you have been praying for your unsaved husband, keep on praying. If you have been praying for a wayward son or daughter, keep on praying. If your marriage is failing, keep on praying. If your wife is struggling, keep on praying. You and I never have the prerogative to quit. We can't give up as long as God is on the throne. Keep asking, seeking, knocking, and praying until you have persisted and God has answered.

*Unto thee will I cry, O Lord my rock;
be not silent to me: lest, if thou be
silent to me, I become like them
that go down into the pit.*

PSALM 28:1

6

When God Is Silent

Have you ever felt totally alone? Have you ever thought, "Where is God when I need Him?" Did the heavens seem silent and there was no immediate answer from God? I'm not talking about those times when you had deliberately sinned against God. I'm talking about those times when you had done all you knew to do that was right and there was still no answer from God.

David apparently faced such a time when he wrote the words of this psalm. He desperately needed to hear from God and cried out for Him not to be silent. In essence he was saying, "God, if I don't hear from you,

I'm going to die!" Such times of spiritual loneliness come, not only when we have failed God, but when we are trying our best to serve Him as well. Perhaps you are going through such a time right now. You are serving the Lord, trusting in Him and walking with Him, but something seems terribly wrong. You are right with God and your fellow man, and yet there is an emptiness inside your heart. Everything seems to be in proper order, but you don't feel the closeness of God like you once did.

I don't know about you, but I have certainly felt that way at times in my life. I knew that Christ lived within my soul and that I was at peace with God, yet I seemed to be wrestling with the whole issue of God's presence in my life. I was busy serving God, yet He seemed to be silent in all my busyness and activity. If you have ever had this experience, you will certainly identify with the pain one sometimes experiences in the pursuit of God.

And in such periods of personal struggle or spiritual depression, we are often reminded that God is still at work in our lives. His sanctifying process is not finished. He is still conforming us to the image of Christ that we might become more like Him.

WHY GOD IS SILENT

There are several reasons for God's silence, and each points to a different aspect of His work of grace on our behalf. Each confronts a different aspect of our spiritual progress, and each is designed to draw us closer to Him.

1. We Are Too Busy to Listen.

There are times that God is silent because we are not listening to what He has to say. He sees all the hustle and bustle in our daily routine and realizes that we wouldn't hear Him even if He did speak to us at that moment. We are often just too busy to hear from God. Our lives are filled with rushing here and there, and we rarely take time to be quiet and seek His face.

Busyness is not Godliness. It may be a necessity of life, but it is an activity that must be controlled or it will control us. All too often we are too busy to pray, too busy for church, and even too busy for our own families. When we allow the busy activities of life to fill our time, they will always drain our souls.

The problem with busyness is that it leaves little time for seeking God. Quiet contemplation is not exactly one of the virtues of modern society. We tend to do more because we have more. All our time-saving conveniences and modern devices only cause us to try to do more instead of less. Since we can go great distances quickly, we are going more but enjoying it less. Today's generation has the best technology the human race has ever known, and yet we are the most miserable generation that has ever lived.

I don't mean to imply that work is wrong. On the contrary, we have a God-given mandate to work. Industriousness and hard work are two virtues which God blesses. But when activity becomes an end in itself, it will usually rob us of personal and spiritual vitality. Sometimes it will even be necessary to restrict our activities in order to spend quiet and quality time with God.

I am convinced that there are times when God is

silent because we are not listening. Recently, I was talking to a man in a very crowded room. I began to express something to him that was heavy upon my heart. I tried my best to arrest his attention, but as I talked, he kept glancing about the crowd of people. His eyes darted everywhere as though he were looking for someone important. He even greeted several people who passed by while I was talking to him—or rather, talking *at* him. Finally, after about five minutes, I gave up in utter frustration. I stopped talking and quietly walked away. Why did I quit? Because he wasn't listening. He didn't really have time for me, and I was wasting my time trying to talk to somebody who wasn't hearing anything I had to say.

Unfortunately, that is how many of us treat God. We are so busy that we don't take time to listen to what He has to say. Our personal relationship with Him is way down at the bottom of our list of priorities. All too often we don't have any real time for God. He desires our fellowship and communion, but we are the problem. Even when we try to take time to pray, we allow the telephone, the doorbell, and even the television to interrupt us.

"Oh, God, I need your help," we often pray. "I need to hear from you right now." Then the phone rings, and we spend the next hour talking about nothing really important. Our real attitude often seems to be saying, "God, I need your help, but I'm so busy, I really don't have time to seek it." We act like God is some kind of celestial bellhop or glorified errand boy to do our bidding. We want Him to fit into our schedule and to operate within our time frame.

We must remember that we are not God. He is God. He alone is sovereign over the events in our lives. He chooses when and how He will answer our prayers, and He will do it in accord with His will, not our wills. Every time we try to rush God, we insult the Holy Spirit and He simply and quietly withdraws His power from our lives.

The Bible reminds us that God will only show Himself "strong in the behalf of them whose heart is perfect toward him" (2 Chronicles 16:9). It also tells us, "And ye shall seek me, and find me, when ye shall search for me with all your heart" (Jeremiah 29:13). Finding God's answers to life's toughest questions is a matter of the heart. Sometimes He is silent because He has found us so busy and rude that He is not about to reveal Himself to us. The least God deserves is our undivided attention. "Be still, and know that I am God" (Psalm 46:10).

2. We Have Already Said No.

There are times when God is silent because He has spoken to us before and we have said no to His will. Therefore, He withholds new direction until we have acted upon the truth we already know. Only when we act upon the truth, do we really prove that we believe it.

I have always been intrigued by the Old Testament story of Jonah. Most of us have heard of his famous ride in the great fish, but few people remember the point of the story. God told Jonah the prophet to go to Nineveh, the capital of Israel's enemy, Assyria. He told him to preach against their sins and call them to repentance. Instead, Jonah turned in the opposite direction and ran to Joppa on the Mediterranean Coast. From there he sailed westward out to sea.

Eventually, a storm arose, and the sailors cast Jonah overboard. He was swallowed by a "great fish" and spent three days and nights in its belly. Can't you just hear him calling out to God in desperation? The Bible says, "Then Jonah prayed to the Lord his God out of the fish's belly" (Jonah 2:1). He cried out for mercy and asked God to deliver him. Yet, for three days and nights there was no answer from God. For all that time God did not speak to the disobedient prophet. When God finally did speak, He spoke not to Jonah but to the *fish,* who finally spit Jonah up upon dry ground! Then God spoke a second time and again told Jonah to go to Nineveh. This time Jonah obeyed, and God used him to bring a great awakening to that pagan city.

Whenever God taps on the door of your heart, you had better be ready to answer His call. If He has spoken to you about a specific matter, He expects you to do it. Don't try to rationalize your way out or explain the whole thing away. If you say no, God may not speak again.

If you are concerned that you already may have rejected God's calling in your life, tell Him that you are ready to obey Him now. Reaffirm your faith in Him, and recommit yourself to doing His will in your life. It is never too late to start over in making things right with God.

3. He Is Putting Our Faith to the Test.
There have been many times in my life when God's silence stretched my faith and caused me to grow in my

walk with God. I may have faced insurmountable obstacles even though I knew my life was right was Him. I could memorize His promises, claim His power, and pray in faith, but He was still silent, and the silence became deafening.

When those times of silence came, all I could do was take hold of the rope of faith, tie a knot in the end, and hang on for dear life. I would then cry out to Him, pray, and claim His promise to never leave me nor forsake me. I had to cast every burden and care upon Him, knowing that His power was sufficient to sustain me.

It is only in those dark and lonely moments that we come to grips with the security and eternalness of our salvation. It is then that we are assured that we are the branches and He is the vine. We have been grafted into Him, and nothing can separate us from the love of God (see Romans 8:28–32).

When all else fails, faith hangs on to the end. The Scripture encourages us to remember that faith is the *substance* of things hoped for and the *evidence* of things not seen (Hebrews 11:1). Faith is the absolute reality of God's presence in our lives, and it enables us to hold on in times when God is silent.

In ancient times there lived a man named Job, who suffered the greatest personal crises imaginable. His property was stolen, his fortune vanished, his children died, his wife turned against him, and he finally was overcome with a serious disease. Everything that could have gone wrong went wrong in his life. Overwhelmed by all this personal tragedy, he collapsed into mourning in a pile of ashes. The Bible describes him as a broken man, covered with boils, scratching himself with a broken piece of pottery. In the depth of his agony, he called upon God but found him silent.

To make things even worse, Job's three friends arrived to console him and ended up condemning him. They assumed that he had sinned against God and was being judged for his sin. Even his wife cried, "Curse God, and die" (Job 2:9). Most of us would have given up at that point. We would have hit the bottom of life's barrel and thrown in the towel of defeat. Yet, despite his anguish of soul, brokenness of spirit, and depth of pain, Job said, "Though he slay me, yet will I trust in him" (Job 13:15).

Job's response to his troubles was to call upon God. When the Almighty did not answer at first, Job said that though God may be silent right now, he would still trust in Him. His faith was being tested. It was being expanded and stretched to the very limits of human endurance. Finally, God restored to him all he had lost and more. Faith is not really tested when all is going well, but only when all is going wrong. Our faith is not increased when life's boat sails calmly on a glassy sea, but when the storms come, the wind blows, and the waves begin to smash our vessel into the rocks of life, then faith grows.

4. God Is Getting Our Attention.

Silence is often deafening! It is so quiet that it shouts at us. Have you ever noticed how quickly silence gets attention? If you have ever been in a noisy room and it suddenly became quiet, chances are that everybody noticed.

God often uses silence to get our attention. When

He has spoken to us time and again and we don't listen, He often resorts to silence. He may withdraw His voice from your soul, so that you will begin searching for Him all the more intently.

Have you ever been in a crowded, noisy room and watched someone standing there in silence? Soon people will approach that person to ask if things are all right with them. "What's wrong?" they may ask. "You're not talking. Are you all right?"

Believe it or not, there is a sound to silence. It speaks louder than a thunderous roar. When God speaks to us through His silence, He inevitably gets our attention. We may have been too preoccupied with our own interests to notice at first, but eventually we realize that God is no longer speaking because we are not listening.

WHAT TO DO WHEN GOD IS SILENT

Since God often uses silence to speak to us, we need to know how to respond to His silence. What should I do when there is seemingly no answer from God? Here are three things to consider.

1. Silence Does Not Mean Separation.

Remember, if you are God's child by faith in Jesus Christ, nothing can permanently separate you from God. Just because He is silent doesn't mean He has departed. The Apostle Paul said, "For I am persuaded, that neither death, nor life, nor angels, nor principalities, nor powers, nor things present, nor things to come, nor height, nor depth, nor any other creature shall be able to separate us from the love of God" (Romans 8:38–39).

Paul had been beaten, stoned, and even left for dead. On more than one occasion, he was imprisoned and punished without trial. If anybody could ever have asked, "Where is God?" it was certainly the Apostle Paul. At times even other Christians questioned why he suffered so much. Unbelievers scorned him, fellow Christians criticized him, and some of his own companions forsook him. Yet, through it all, Paul knew that Christ was real and that His will could be trusted.

2. *Silence Does Not Mean Denial.*

God's silence does not necessarily mean that the answer to our prayers is no. He may be silent so that I will become motivated to deal with my own shortcomings. In the long run, His silence may actually stretch my faith in God.

Recently, my wife and I were sitting in a restaurant. We noticed a young mother with her small son sitting at a table nearby. The boy seemed to be about six years old, yet his mother was cutting his food for him and feeding it to him piece by piece. I thought to myself how that was a disservice to that youngster. She was cheating him out of maturing on his own. He needed to learn to use a knife and fork for himself. Her well-intended efforts were only frustrating the growth process which needed to occur in the boy's life.

The late Oswald J. Smith was one of the great missionary-minded pastors of the twentieth century. As a young man, he wanted to go to the mission field, but God never gave him any specific direction. He was willing to go to Africa, Asia, or wherever God might want to send him. Since God remained silent, Dr. Smith went to Toronto, Canada, to establish the People's Church. Instead of sending him to a specific field, God led him to build the greatest missionary-sending-and-supporting church of our time. Today there are thousands of missionaries encircling the globe because God was silent to a young preacher named Oswald J. Smith.

3. Silence Does Not Mean God Is Finished.

God may be silent because He is in the midst of doing a great work in our behalf. Be reminded that the very purpose for His working now is to conform us into the image of His Son, Jesus Christ. And that, my friend, in most of our lives is quite a task! Will He give up on us? No, not according to the Scriptures. Philippians 1:6 says, "Being confident of this very thing, that he which hath begun a good work in you will perform it until the day of Jesus Christ." Yes, for the moment He may be silent, but even in His silence He is working, waiting for the precise moment to speak His words of direction to our hearts again. Our task is to listen and in childlike obedience make the moves He commands when He does speak.

At the early part of the last century, an artist who was also a great chess player painted a picture of a chess game. The two players were a young man and Satan. The young man was given the white pieces and Satan the black. The issue of the game was this: Should the young man win, he was forever free from the power of evil; should the Devil win, the young man was to be his slave forever. The artist evidently believed in the supreme power of evil, for his picture portrayed Satan as the victor.

In the conception of the artist, the Devil had just moved his queen and had announced a checkmate in four moves. The young man's hand was pictured hovered over his rook; his face paled with fear—there was no hope. The Devil had won! The young man was to be a slave to evil forever.

For many years this picture hung in a great art gallery in Cincinnati, Ohio. Chess players from all over the world came to view the picture. With every conceivable move they tried to help the young man, but to no avail. They hated the thought of the artist that the Devil wins.

After several years it was concluded that there was one chess player on earth who could prove the artist wrong. That man was the aged Paul Morphy, a resident of New Orleans, who was the supreme master of chess in his day, an undefeated champion. He had retired from the game due to the mental strain. A plan was arranged to bring Morphy to Cincinnati to view the picture.

After he arrived, as he stood before the picture, two mighty impulses arose in his mind: first, that which leads a brave man to take the role of an underdog; second, that which resents the passing of a crown of supremacy which has not been challenged.

Morphy stood and viewed the painting five minutes, ten minutes, twenty minutes, thirty minutes. He was all concentration; he lifted his hand and lowered it, as in his imagination he made and eliminated moves. Suddenly, his hand paused, his eyes burned with the vision of a previously unthought-of combination. Then loudly he shouted, "Young man, make that move. That's the move! That's the move!"

To the amazement of all, the old master, the *supreme chess personality,* had discovered a combination that the creating artist had not considered. The way out was there all the time. The young man could defeat the Devil. The supreme master had restored hope to all who viewed the picture.

Our lives are much like that of this young man. On our own we have little hope against Satan's powers. But the great assurance is that even when it seems God is silent, He is still there, viewing our lives, waiting for the moment to speak to us His *divine directives,* which always result in victory.

*Verily, verily, I say unto you, whatsoever
ye shall ask the Father in my name,
he will give it to you. Hitherto have ye
asked nothing in my name: ask, and ye
shall receive, that your joy may be full.*

JOHN 16:23–24

7

Praying in Jesus' Name

When I was a child, I often heard people end their
prayers by saying, "In Jesus' name, Amen." I thought
that was a nice, logical conclusion to their prayers.
It seemed to me to work like "signing off" at the end of
a broadcast. But I later learned that praying in Jesus'
name is the most important thing we can say in our
prayers. The name of Jesus is the very key to answered
prayer.

You can pray without mentioning Jesus' name if you
like, but you are missing out on the great power of
prayer if you do. You can pray "for Jesus' sake" if you
like, but prayer is not for His sake; it is for our sake.
Praying in His name means that we are praying by His

authority and in the power of His Person. In fact, our Lord Himself taught us to pray in His name. He also promised great results if we would do just that.

In the ancient world, official requests were carried by hand and delivered in person. Those requests which were written as royal decrees carried the royal insignia. Those decrees which were delivered verbally were always given "in the name of" or "by the authority of" some prominent leader. This is the significance of praying in Jesus' name. Using His name acknowledges His Lordship and authority in our lives.

PRIORITY OF JESUS' NAME

Jesus is the name for "savior." *Jesus* is the Greek name in the New Testament which translates the Old Testament Hebrew name *Joshua*, which means "savior" or "deliverer." It is the perfect name for Christ since He, like the Old Testament leader, Joshua, was the leader of His people. The term *Christ* is taken from the Greek *christos*, meaning "anointed one" or "messiah." Thus, Jesus is our Lord's personal name and Christ is His title.

The importance of Jesus' name is emphasized in Scripture, which says, "Wherefore God also hath highly exalted him, and given him a name which is above every name: That at the name of Jesus every knee should bow . . . and that every tongue should confess that Jesus Christ is Lord, to the glory of God the Father" (Philippians 2:10–11).

I have news for you. Everyone will one day acknowledge the Lordship and authority of Christ. The communist leaders of Russia will be forced to acknowledge Him. The cultic followers of Sun Myong Moon, the "moonies," will bow down before Him. The Buddhists, Moslems, Hindus, and all the rest will kneel before Jesus Christ and proclaim Him King of Kings and Lord of Lords.

There are many things about the name of Jesus that make His name so very special.

1. Jesus Is a Name from Heaven.

The Bible tells us that the angel who appeared to Mary told her what to name the baby. He said, "Behold, thou shalt conceive in thy womb, and bring forth a son, and shalt call his name Jesus" (Luke 1:31). God chose His name and sent His angel to announce that name.

Parents love to name their children. Even when we can't agree on the name, we enjoy giving it. I wanted to name my little girl Elizabeth and call her "Liz," but my wife, Judy, preferred calling her "Libby." I didn't like the sound of Libby Lee, and she didn't like the sound of Liz Lee; so we named her Tonya Elizabeth and called her Tonya. That selection certainly proved best!

The significance of Jesus' name, however, was that God Himself selected it. The name for "savior" was the perfect name for God's incarnate Son. The Bible says of that name, "Neither is there salvation in any other: for there is none other name under heaven given among men, whereby we must be saved" (Acts 4:12). No other name, not Edward, Richard, James, or Robert, can bring salvation. Only the name of Jesus can save.

2. Jesus Is a Name of Hope.

God sent His Son into the world to give us the hope of heaven and eternal life. The angel promised Joseph that the child born to Mary would "save his people from their sins" (Matthew 1:21). The Apostle Peter said, "Whosoever shall call on the name of the Lord shall be saved" (Acts 2:21), and the Apostle Paul said the same thing in Romans 10:13.

No other name can bring such hope of forgiveness and deliverance from sin. There is power in the name of Jesus. His is a name of hope that brings confidence and reassurance to the hearts of people.

One of my responsibilities as a pastor is to visit those in the hospital. Whenever I visit with someone there, I inevitably ask, "Who is your doctor?" I am amazed to discover that everyone seems to think he or she has the best doctor in Atlanta. "Pastor, I hear that he is the best doctor in town," they will often say. I've never yet met someone who told me theirs was the "worst doctor in town." They brag about the doctor, the hospital, and the nurses.

But when I mention the name of Jesus, all other names pale into insignificance. He alone brings a sparkle to the eyes and joy to the heart. The very mention of His name causes a smile to come to their lips and a ray of hope into their hearts. Whenever I get down or discouraged, I whisper the name of Jesus, and hope swells up in my heart as well.

3. Jesus Is a Name of Honor.

Jesus' name is associated with victory and deliverance. Just as Joshua, His Old Testament namesake, conquered the Promised Land and drove out Israel's enemies, so Jesus has conquered Satan's power and given us eternal life in heaven. As Joshua marched through the land of Canaan, his very name brought the hope of deliverance to the Israelites and struck fear in the hearts of their enemies.

The demons trembled before Jesus Christ. "What have we to do with thee?" they cried. Satan could not tempt Him to sin. Rome could not conquer Him. The scribes could not outwit Him. Even the crucifixion could not stop Him. Jesus came to this earth to die for our sins and rise again the third day. In so doing, He trampled underfoot the very head of Satan himself, opening the way for all who choose to live the joyful Christian life.

A young man in our church recently said, "Pastor, I don't know what to do; it's just getting better all the time." As he talked about his faith in Christ and his relationship with Him, tears of joy trickled down his face.

"You don't have to worry about what to do," I replied. "Just go ahead and enjoy it!"

We don't have to wait to get to heaven to enjoy our salvation. We have already been made citizens of the heavenly kingdom. We have eternal life within our hearts. The Promised Land is already in our possession, and we need to live our spiritual lives to the fullest extent.

> Jesus too had a Promised Land,
> It wasn't a place,
> It was a plan.

It is unfortunate that some Christians think that they have to be miserable in order to be spiritual. Jesus said, "I am come that they might have life, and that they might have it more abundantly" (John 10:10). He has an abundant plan for each of our lives, and He is unfolding that plan every step of the way.

POWER OF JESUS' NAME

When our Lord Jesus taught on the subject of prayer, He urged His disciples to pray in His name (John 16:23). In so doing, He was emphasizing the power and authority of His name. He even went so far as to promise that He would give us whatever we ask in His name.

I like that word *whatever*. My imagination runs wild with that kind of promise. I can remember sitting in school as a boy and imagining that I was fishing on a pond or playing basketball at camp. My imagination transcended the mundane matters at hand and transported me into another realm. That is what happens when I grasp this promise about prayer. Whatever I ask in His name and according to His will shall come to reality because it is asked in His authority.

Whenever we ask according to His will, we can be sure that He will answer us. Thus, there should be a humble confidence about Christian prayer. It is not presumption nor is it total passivity. Prayer is neither passive nor presumptuous. It is the expression of faith within our hearts.

We cannot pray selfishly to fulfill our own carnal desires. For example, you can't ask in faith for someone else's money or possessions. God's power to answer our prayers is limited by His sinless nature. It is a divinely-imposed self-limitation. In other words, God will not do wrong in order to appease our fleshly desires.

In the Book of Acts, we read of the time when Peter and John were entering the temple and a beggar stopped them. Moved with compassion, Peter said, "Silver and gold have I none, but such as I have give I thee: In the name of Jesus Christ of Nazareth, rise up and walk" (Acts 3:6). The man was helped up and began "walking and leaping and praising God." The power to heal him had been communicated in Jesus' name.

Peter's response to the beggar was in direct obedience to Christ's command to ask *all things* in His name. Later, when Peter was questioned by the authorities, he told them that this miracle had been done in the name of Jesus. "And his name, through faith in his name, hath made this man strong," Peter replied (Acts 3:16). Therefore, Peter appealed to his entire audience to repent and be saved (3:19).

Peter knew that the risen Christ had ascended to heaven and was seated at the Father's right hand in the place of power and authority. He knew that he could pray with confidence in the power of Jesus' name.

PRIVILEGE OF JESUS' NAME

The name of Jesus is not something to be used lightly. The Bible warns us against taking God's name in vain, which means asking God to do something that we have no right to ask. In fact, our Lord had to authorize His disciples to pray in His name. "Hitherto you have asked nothing in my name," He told them, and then He commanded them to pray in His name.

Our Lord was near the end of His earthly ministry. He would soon go to the cross on Calvary's hill to shed His blood for our sins. The power of His atonement and His victorious resurrection conquered sin and death. While He had always been the Lamb of God slain for our sins from the foundation of earth in the mind of God, He then triumphed over sin and sealed our redemption on the cross.

After His resurrection, Jesus ascended into heaven, where He makes intercession for us to the Father. He personally expresses our prayers to God the Father and serves as our advocate in heaven. It is there that He serves as our great High Priest.

Prior to Jesus' death on the cross, sins were temporarily covered by the offering of animal sacrifices at the temple. There a great curtain or veil separated the inner sanctuary of the Holy of Holies from the rest of the temple. Ordinary people were never permitted to go beyond that veil. It separated men from God. Only on the Day of Atonement (Yom Kippur) could the High Priest himself enter through the curtain to make atonement for the sins of Israel. He alone was permitted access only after he had properly washed and robed himself.

In the Holy of Holies, the High Priest stood before the presence of God at the Ark of the Covenant. Jewish historians tell us that the people even tied a rope around the High Priest's leg so that in the event he died in the presence of God, they could pull him out without entering themselves.

Mark 15:38 states that when Jesus died on the cross, the veil of the temple was split in two from top to bottom. One historian tells us that veil was one hundred feet high and nine feet thick. God split it wide open to signify that access into His presence was now made possible by the atoning blood of Jesus Christ.

From that point on, God has given each one of us the privilege of coming directly into His presence. We do not have to come through any priest or human mediator of any kind. We can now come boldly before the throne of grace to obtain help in time of need because Jesus made it possible.

What a privilege! We can come directly into God's presence because of Jesus' atonement for our sins. Before you lay your head on your pillow tonight, you can come into God's presence through the privilege of prayer. Someone wrote:

> Not all the blood of beasts
> On Jewish altars slain,
> Could give the guilty conscience peace
> Or wash away the stain.
>
> But Jesus the heavenly Lamb,
> Takes all our sins away.
> A sacrifice of nobler name
> And richer blood than they.

PURPOSE OF JESUS' NAME

What is the purpose of praying in Jesus' name? Our Lord Himself answered that question when He said, "Ask, and ye shall receive, that your joy may be full"

(John 16:24). He wants to fill your life with the joy of His presence and power. He is delighted when we come to Him asking by faith in His name.

When a Christian has enough faith to bring his burdens and needs to the Savior, he is really saying, "Lord Jesus, I know that you love me and that you care about my problems." Our prayers in His name express our confidence in His character and our faith in His desire to meet our needs.

As we pray to God the Father, Jesus receives those prayers and expresses them to the Father. He might receive a prayer of mine and say, "Father, it's Richard again. He is praying for people to be saved today at Rehoboth Church."

"What gives him the authority to ask for this?" the Father might ask.

"He is asking it in my name," our Lord replies.

"Then let it be done," comes the Father's reply.

Never become weary in praying. Don't make the mistake of thinking you are bothering God with your requests. Every time you pray in Jesus' name, you are invoking the power of heaven on your behalf. Remember, the Bible says, "Ye have not, because ye ask not" (James 4:2). Start asking in Jesus' name, and see what happens. And remember, when you pray in His name, you are invoking His authority.

And this is the confidence that we have in him, that, if we ask any thing according to his will, he heareth us: And if we know that he hear us, whatsoever we ask, we know that we have the petitions that we desired of him.

1 JOHN 5:14–15

8

Getting Prayers Answered

Getting results from prayer is one of our greatest concerns. Recently a man came to me and asked me to pray that he would get a certain position at work. "I really want that position," he announced abruptly. "I am praying that I will get it."

We prayed together and several weeks passed before I saw him again. "Did you get the job?" I asked.

"I really prayed for that job," he replied, "but *just like I expected,* somebody else got it instead."

I thought to myself, "You really got what you prayed for because what you expected is what you got!"

Too many of us treat prayer as if it were a routine

spin of chance. "If I am lucky," we think, "maybe God will say yes this time." Unfortunately, that kind of half-hearted praying is going on all the time.

The Bible promises us that if we pray properly, we can be confident that God will answer us according to His will for our lives. Prayer is the most powerful force in our lives. It expresses the need of the human soul and touches the very heart of God Himself. Prayer is the most dynamic force available to us, and yet few of us really pray. Those who have not learned to pray are still living on the carnal level of life. They are missing the greatest spiritual power they could ever know.

Only as we pray in faith will we begin to see God at work in our lives. Each of us must be willing to take God at His word and believe that He can do what He has promised to do for us. The God who can stop the sun or part the Red Sea can certainly answer our prayers.

I have found several key truths in Scripture that have made prayer work for me. I want to share them with you so they can work for you as well.

UNDERSTAND GOD'S PROMISES

The promises of God are clearly stated in Scripture. The key to obtaining them is faith. Jesus said, "All things are possible to him that believeth" (Mark 9:23). That is a promise of unlimited potential. Our ability to get our prayers answered is measured by our faith in God.

Faith is confidence in the integrity of God's promises. When we pray in faith, we are telling God that we trust His integrity. We are expressing that confidence by the very act of prayer itself. When we pray, we are communicating with the infinite and personal God who controls the entire universe. When you understand that, it takes the surprise out of answered prayer.

"Guess what, pastor?" people will often say, "God answered my prayer!" They sound so surprised that I am often disappointed. We ought to believe that He is going to answer our prayers and expect Him to do it!

Answered prayer is not so much a miracle as it is a fulfillment of God's spiritual laws. He has already promised that if we pray "according to His will," He will grant our requests. This is a divine principle that always works. If my prayer is in submission to His will, I am going to get my prayer answered.

"What if I am asking for something that is not His will?" you may ask. Remember, if it isn't His will for your life, you don't really want it. When I am willing to submit my desires to His plan and purpose, my life takes on even greater meaning and significance.

When I come to God in prayer in submission to His will, I am placing the greatest possible faith in His integrity. That kind of praying says, "God, I trust you with my life even more than I trust myself!"

Faith is not desire. Some people only pray for the things they desire, like a new house or a new car. Praying by faith is the kind of prayer that says, "God, let me know your will about the car."

The *prayer of faith* trusts God to do what is best about the car. The *prayer of desire* says, "God, give me that car!" If we don't get it, we end up mad at God. That is not the prayer of faith, and God's refusal to answer it is not a failure on His part.

Prayer is also more than just positive thinking. I like positive thinkers. But positive thinking alone is no replacement for genuine prayer. I have often heard people say that they thought God was going to do something simply because *they* thought so. But that is not how God operates. We cannot force God to do things our way just because we think it is best for us.

When I was a little boy, we had another boy in our neighborhood who thought he was Superman. He had a very positive attitude about this belief. He even convinced his mother to buy him some blue leotards and make him a red cape with a yellow chest patch with a big red "S" on it. He went around the neighborhood telling everyone that he was Superman. He was as positive and optimistic as he could be. In fact, he was so convincing that some of the children began to believe him.

"I'm Superman!" the boy insisted to everyone he met. But the day of reckoning eventually came. One day another boy said, "If you are Superman, prove it!"

Caught in his own delusion, the boy insisted that he really was Superman.

"Then let's see you fly," replied his challenger. Tragically, little Superman climbed up on the neighbor's rooftop and jumped off in an attempt to fly. He hit the ground with a thud and broke his arm! All the positive thinking he had done could not prevent his inevitable "collision" with the fact that he was not Superman.

Unfortunately, many people treat God the same way. They think God is going to perform for them in a certain manner just because they think He ought to do it that way. We can beg, scheme, manipulate, and all the rest, but if our request is not in accordance with God's will for our lives, He won't answer it. Real faith is simply believing that God will answer our prayers according to His will. It involves our placing our trust in His integrity. Such prayer is the expression of our confidence in His character and our reliance upon His good intentions on our behalf.

DISCOVER GOD'S DIRECTION

If the answer to our prayers must be in accord with God's will for our lives, then it is imperative that we clearly understand His will in any given situation. Fortunately, God does not leave the knowledge of His will up to guesswork. He has written a book explaining His will in great detail. That book is *the Bible.* Holy and sacred to Jews and Christians alike, the Bible clearly explains the will of God for the basic issues of life.

The discovery of God's will rests upon our clear understanding of the content and context of Scripture. The whole Word of God is the expression of His will and purpose for our lives. Therefore, every verse of Scripture must be interpreted in light of its context and in relation to the rest of Scripture. None of us has the right to take any passage out of context and attempt to interpret it for ourselves without viewing it in relation to the rest of revealed truth.

The Apostle Paul wrote, "All scripture is given by inspiration of God, and is profitable for doctrine, for reproof, for correction, for instruction in righteousness: That the man of God may be perfect, thoroughly furnished unto all good works" (2 Timothy 3:16–17). Therefore, all sixty-six books of the Bible and each of the 1,189 chapters are inspired by God. Thus, the Bible is God's manual for successful living.

Before we ever begin praying, we need to refer to the instructional manual. Check the directions to see if you are moving in the right manner. Make sure your prayers are consistent with God's revealed truth. He won't answer a prayer that contradicts His own principles.

We also need the guidance of *the Holy Spirit* in order to understand God's will for our lives. Jesus said, "Howbeit when he, the Spirit of truth, is come, he will guide you into all truth" (John 16:13). The Holy Spirit dwells in every believer's mind and heart. He uses the truth of Scripture to instruct, guide, convict, and encourage us in our daily walk with God. He leads us intuitively in the way we should go.

This does not mean that the Holy Spirit will lead us contrary to Scripture. Rather He will guide us to the truth of Scripture that it might direct our lives in the way of the Lord. Remember, the will of God will always be consistent with the Word of God.

We also discover the will of God by developing *a sanctified mind.* As our minds are spiritually cleansed and renewed, they are proper receptacles for God's truth. You will never discover the will of God by reading secular magazines or by watching secular television. Advice from the best secular minds falls far short of the revealed truth of the Word of God.

Finally, we also find the will of God through *the doors of opportunity* which He opens to us. God is the One who opens and closes those doors for us. If a door of service is closed to you, then you can be sure that is not God's will for your life. If a door of service is open to you, that may well be His will for you. I say that with some reserve, realizing that God may open two or three doors of opportunity at the same time and you will have to choose one of them. Among those that are open to you, there may be more than one that is acceptable in His will, and you must choose between them. Most of us, however, don't have the privilege of more than one door open at a time, and it becomes evident that the one door of opportunity we have is indeed His will for us.

Sometimes it is not so important *who* you are as *where* you are in relation to finding God's will. It is more important that you be in the right place for Him to use you. I remember hearing a story several years ago about a state governor who went to visit a state mental hospital. While he was there, he needed to make a telephone call and asked to use a phone. He dialed the operator and said, "Hello, this is the governor. Please give me an outside line."

When the operator didn't answer, the governor began raising his voice and demanding an outside line.

Finally, in desperation, the governor asked, "Do you know who I am? This is the governor!"

To which the operator responded, "I don't know *who* you are, but I do know *where* you are!"

I wonder how long it has been since you put yourself in a proper place to hear from God? How long has it been since you searched the Scriptures and asked the Holy Spirit to reveal God's will for your life? How long has it been since you fasted and prayed and gave yourself totally over to God?

It is only by this kind of determined search that we can discover God's perfect will for our specific lives. Don't give up the quest. Keep seeking; keep knocking; and keep searching. Remember, "This is the confidence that we have in him, that, if we ask any thing according to his will, he heareth us" (1 John 5:14).

SEARCH FOR GOD'S ILLUMINATION

There is nothing more frustrating than fumbling around in the dark. Sometimes it seems that is just what we are doing while we are searching for the light of God's direction. A young businessman recently asked me, "Pastor, what can I do if I have read the Scripture, prayed fervently, and waited patiently for an answer to my prayers, and nothing seems to happen?"

I reminded him that there are times when we have done all we know to do and must be willing to pray in the light of truth that we have already. I may not know the totality of God's direction for my life, but I do know that I am moving ahead in the light I already have for now.

When the Babylonian King Nebuchadnezzar commanded the Israelites to bow before his golden statue, three young Hebrews refused to do so. When Shadrach, Meshach, and Abednego stood their ground, they were threatened with being thrown into a fiery furnace. But in spite of their own fears, they replied, "If it be so, our God whom we serve is able to deliver us from the burning fiery furnace, and he will deliver us out of thy hand, O King. But if not, be it known unto thee, O King, that we will not serve thy gods, nor worship the golden image which thou hast set up" (Daniel 3:17–18).

Notice that these young men would not presume on the will of God. They were prepared to accept either option: life or death. Either would have been a form of deliverance from the wrath of the king. Both options were possible, and they were willing to accept either one in the will of God for their lives. They were trusting God's integrity and leaving the consequences in His hands.

During the War Between the States, Confederate General Robert E. Lee went into a church and knelt to pray. When he left the church, someone asked him if he were praying for the South to win the war. But the general looked at him and simply said, "No, I wasn't praying for us to win. I was praying that God's will would be done." Now that's the way to pray!

Prayer is not an easy process even though there may be times when it seems easy to pray. For there will also come difficult times when it is hard to pray. Such times will test your faith and stretch you to the limits of your humanity. But when you can pray even in the face of adversity, "Lord, not my will, but thine be done," you can rest assured God will answer with that which is best for you.

Charles Spurgeon, the great Baptist pastor in the last century, said, "We may not always be able to trace the hand of God, but we can always trust the heart of God."

How can we be assured of getting our prayers answered? By learning to pray in faith. The key to answered prayer is a believing heart. The rest is up to God! Once we learn to pray understanding His promises and discovering His direction, the rest is a matter of trusting the light of revelation we have and walking by faith.

Prayer is a matter of the heart. It is the cry of a newborn child of God. It is the call for help when we are in trouble. It is the confident trust that we learn as mature believers. Praying is as natural to a Christian as breathing is to a baby. It is the heart of man calling out to the heart of God.

Part Three

WHEN THE HEART IS HURTING

My flesh and my heart faileth: but God is the strength of my heart, and my portion forever.

PSALM 73:26

*And forgive us our debts, as we forgive
our debtors. . . . For if ye forgive men
their trespasses, your heavenly Father
will also forgive you: But if ye forgive
not men their trespasses, neither will
your Father forgive your trespasses.*

MATTHEW 6:12, 14–15

9

Why We Must Forgive

The Lord's Prayer is recorded in the sixth chapter of Matthew. It is the most important prayer recorded in all of Scripture because it serves as a model prayer for all Christians. In that prayer (vv. 9–13), our Lord expressed six petitions:

1. Hallowed be thy name.
2. Thy Kingdom come.
3. Thy will be done in earth as it is in heaven.
4. Give us this day our daily bread.

5. And forgive us our debts as we forgive our debtors.

6. And lead us not into temptation, but deliver us from evil.

At the conclusion of His teaching on prayer, Jesus commented on only one of these petitions—the one regarding forgiveness. Perhaps He returned to this petition because it is so foreign to human nature to forgive. Perhaps He felt it needed an explanation and even a warning to those who chose to neglect it. It is interesting that Christ did not comment on the other petitions but concentrated His attention on this one.

You may be thinking of someone who has wronged you, and you have never forgiven him or her. Perhaps he or she has hurt you, wronged you, cheated you, or misrepresented you in some way. Perhaps he or she hurt your wife, husband, or children. You may have tried to forgive that person but cannot.

"You just don't understand what they have done to me," people have often said to me. "I just can't forgive them!" Sometimes the hurt is so deep that it has turned to revenge. "I can't let them get away with this!" they will say. Others will ask pointedly, "Why should I have to forgive them?"

There are several reasons why it is important to forgive. A lack of forgiveness is often indicative of deep-seated bitterness which robs the spiritual vitality of the soul. The great problem with bitterness is that it spreads like a plague until it affects every relationship in our lives.

FORGIVENESS CURES THE
SICKNESS OF THE SOUL

A lack of forgiveness is a spiritual sickness. Its roots run deep, and its branches reach far into the hearts of men. If you are an unforgiving person, you are a spiritually sick person. The roots of anger, bitterness, jealousy, guilt, and hatred will torment your soul and twist your life out of control.

If you have an unforgiving heart, it will be impossible for you to live an effective Christian life. Once you look at life through the eyes of bitterness, you will never see it in proper focus or perspective. For example, if you are a single person who has been jilted by someone else, you may look at love in a negative manner. "I'll only love again with reservations," people often say after a heartbreaking romance. "I'm not going to get hurt like that again," they often insist. What such people are really saying is that they have not forgiven that person and they are letting bitterness control their lives.

The violation of trust always hurts. Perhaps you have been financially defrauded by someone. He or she made certain promises but never came through for you. You trusted him or her with an investment or maybe even with your life savings, and that person let you down. Now you have a bitterness toward him or her in the subconscious of your mind. Your resentment and hostility may appear suppressed to others, but it is running rampant in your soul.

If you don't get over your bitterness, you will never be able to trust anyone again. You will question everyone's motives and wonder what hidden agenda is really behind their attitudes and actions. You will begin to develop the kind of paranoia that motivates one to "do unto others, before they get a chance to do it unto you!"

Once our lives become clouded with bitterness and resentment, it is impossible for us to enjoy life itself. Bitterness not only keeps us from forgiving, but it also keeps us from living. Bitter people cannot love, laugh, or enjoy life. They become embroiled in self-pity and destructive self-centeredness. Once you decide not to forgive, you are destined to a second or third-rate existence as a human being. Such inner turmoil will lead to self-torment and emotional anguish. You will play the incidents of your bitterness over and over like a broken record until you become spiritually and emotionally drained.

I once heard of a Greek legend about a man who was tormented by a strange veiled figure. Every time the man sat down to a meal, the veiled figure would appear out of the darkness and steal his food. Every time he was about to attain happiness or success, the veiled figure would appear and snatch it away.

Finally, the man became determined to find out his tormentor's identity. He waited until the precise moment when the strange figure appeared and grabbed the tormenter by the veil. As they struggled together, the man pulled back the veil only to discover that the face of the tormenter was that of his own!

Many of us are our own worst enemies. Our unforgiving spirit eats away at our spiritual vitality until we self-destruct. The Bible says, "He that is slow to anger is better than the mighty; and he that ruleth his spirit than he that taketh a city" (Proverbs 16:32). In other words, the person who can rule over himself is greater than one who can conquer a city. Self-discipline and self-control are two of the greatest assets we can develop.

I have seen people who claim to know Christ and to possess eternal salvation who are filled with resentment and bitterness. Some of them even claim to be filled with the Holy Spirit, but in reality they are filled with hostility and revenge. They may indeed know the Savior but not the joy of His salvation.

Such people are never truly free. Their spirit is bound in the chains of bitterness. They cannot live life or love others as they ought because their hearts are heavy with guilt.

Booker T. Washington was a famous black educator who was often criticized and maligned by his peers in the white community. They argued that he would never succeed in reaching a high standard of education or in building a quality institution. But Washington was a man who had a deep faith in Christ. He had God in his life and knew that He could overcome every obstacle before him.

"I will never allow any man to destroy or denigrate my soul by making me hate him," Washington said.

Whenever we allow ourselves to become consumed with hate, we will eventually become like the object of our bitterness. Our hatred does not destroy others; it only destroys us. You are only hurting yourself if you refuse to forgive those who have hurt you. We need to forgive in order to rid ourselves of spiritual sickness in our souls.

FORGIVENESS HELPS US FORGET

The phrase "forgive and forget" is a well-known, popular saying. It is often repeated, and some people even have it inscribed on a plague hanging on their walls. But the concept of "forgive and forget" is much easier to recite than it is to perform. Many people claim to have forgiven someone, but then add, "But I just can't forget!"

Forgiving and forgetting have to go hand in hand if they are to work properly. It is impossible to truly forgive without forgetting, and it is impossible to forget without forgiving. You may put the offense out of your mind temporarily but hide it away in your heart, and it will still rise to the surface at times in your life.

You may have been wronged by your wife or husband and said, "I forgive you," but ever since you really don't love them as fully as you did before. Some couples think they have forgiven each other and are still filled with resentment years later over an incident that the other one thinks is long forgotten.

Whenever our spirits become restricted toward another person, it is because we are still harboring resentment toward him or her. We cannot fully love others if we are unwilling to forgive them thoroughly and completely. True forgiveness is an issue of the heart. It must begin internally before it can work externally.

Some years ago I read the life story of Corrie Ten Boom, that great Christian woman who was put in a Nazi concentration camp during World War II for hiding Jews in her home. She tells us the terrible and degrading experiences she had to endure in that concentration camp. She even told of the times the S.S. guard would take her from her cell, walk her down a hallway to the shower, and make her strip naked in front of him and take a shower. Then he would stand there watching her, making vulgar and degrading remarks to her the whole time.

Corrie's experiences in that concentration camp were terrible—almost beyond imagination. Her own sister died in that camp, but Corrie lived to tell of her experiences after the war. Rather than becoming bitter, she traveled all over Europe as a spokesperson for forgiveness. She urged Christians to forgive those who had done harm to them during the war.

One day, while speaking on forgiveness in Munich, Corrie finished her talk and descended the platform to address the people who had gathered to meet her. They shook her hand and told her what her message had meant to them. Eventually, a man approached her with his hand extended toward her. At first she did not recognize him, but when he spoke she immediately knew his voice.

"God's forgiveness is good, isn't it?" he said.

As Corrie looked into his eyes, she realized he was the same S.S. guard who had mocked her in the concentration camp years earlier.

"I thought in my heart I had forgiven him," she wrote. "But as he reached out his hand, my hand froze by my side. I could not reach out to him. Here I was, a world-famous forgiver, and I had come face to face with a man I couldn't touch. I prayed to God," she continues, "'God, forgive my inability to forgive.' When I asked God for that, He gave me grace and

I reached out and took his hand and said, 'Yes, God is good.'"*

Corrie realized, in that moment of confrontation, that she had removed the incident from her conscious mind but she had never fully removed it from her heart. She learned in that moment what each of us needs to learn—that forgiveness is a matter of the heart. We must not merely forgive with our lips, but with our hearts. Only then can we truly forget and live above the offenses of others.

FORGIVENESS REMINDS US THAT GOD IS IN CHARGE

Whenever we get hurt by someone else, we are usually quick to judge that person's motives or intentions. But God reminds us that we do not have the final verdict in the matter. We are not God. He alone knows the hearts of men, and He alone can render proper judgment. We cannot possibly know all the motives, circumstances, and backgrounds of those who have hurt us. Therefore, we must be willing to forgive and leave judgment up to God.

My grandmother used to put it like this:

> There's so much bad in the best of us
> And so much good in the worst of us,
> That it ill behooves any of us
> To criticize the rest of us.

* As quoted in *Growing Pains of the Soul* by Joel Gregory (Dallas: Word, 1987), p. 114.

None of us is above reproach. The Bible clearly reminds us, "For all have sinned, and come short of the glory of God" (Romans 3:23). None of us will reach absolute perfection this side of heaven, and none of us will ever be omniscient enough to know everything about everyone else; therefore, we are incapable of rendering final judgment on any matter.

This is not to say that people can wrong others and simply get away with it. Not at all! God said, "Vengeance is mine; I will repay, saith the Lord" (Romans 12:19). God will hold every action in our lives accountable to His righteous standard of judgment. One day He will balance the scales and recompense the evil done against us by others.

Forgiveness can only be effective when it rests on the promise of God's judgment. We don't have to do the judging of others. God will take care of that. Our responsibility is to cleanse our own souls by forgiving those who have wronged us while having confidence that God will properly deal with them.

Forgiveness is also the key to getting our prayers answered. If we don't believe that God is really in control of our lives, we are not going to pray with faith and fervor because an unforgiving heart is an untrusting heart. We cannot forgive others unless we truly trust God.

Forgiveness also reminds us that we have not been given the right to judge others. In fact, our willingness to forgive is our way of trusting God to do the judging. We don't have to worry about getting even because God keeps the books, and He knows what He is doing. We need to concentrate on keeping our hearts right and leave justice up to God.

FORGIVENESS UNLOCKS THE DOOR
TO ANSWERED PRAYER

Our willingness to forgive others is directly related to God's willingness to answer our prayers. In Mark 11:22–26, we read one of the most amazing statements in all of Scripture. Our Lord Jesus said, "Have faith in God. For verily I say unto you, That whosoever shall say unto this mountain, Be thou removed, and be thou cast into the sea; and shall not doubt in his heart, but shall believe that those things which he saith shall come to pass; he shall have whatsoever he saith. Therefore I say unto you, What things soever ye desire, when ye pray, believe that ye receive them, and ye shall have them."

This is undoubtedly one of Jesus' greatest promises. He tells us that the power of prayer is linked to the power of *faith.* The answers to our prayers are related to the extent of our willingness to believe His promises.

But then Jesus added a further condition. He also made it clear that our ability to get our prayers answered is also directly related to *forgiveness.* He said, "And when ye stand praying, forgive, if ye have ought against any: that your Father also which is in heaven may forgive you your trespasses. But if ye do not forgive, neither will your Father which is in heaven forgive your trespasses" (v. 25–26).

There can be little doubt that forgiveness is necessary if we are to get prayers answered. How can we expect God to hear our prayers when we are unwilling to forgive those who have wronged us? After all, we have wronged Him and sinned against Him. We can even pray with great faith and still not get prayers answered because unforgiveness is a sin and it hinders our own relationship to God. He is under no compulsion to respond to an unforgiving heart.

It is interesting to note that in 1 Peter 3:7, the Bible tells husbands that their prayers will not be answered if they do not have a proper relationship with their wives. Husbands are told to *understand* their wives, to *honor* them, and to *share* the grace of life with them, "that your prayers be not hindered." You may be struggling with problems in your business, your personal life, your finances, or even problems with your children because you have failed to meet your wife's needs.

God remains silent because you have not honored your wife. In most cases where tension exists in a marriage, it is because one or both partners have failed to forgive the other. The greatest dishonor we can show each other is to be unforgiving.

Unforgiveness disqualifies us for a life of faith and a life of prayer. Unforgiveness is our way of telling God that we really don't trust Him to do what is right. Perhaps you have prayed for something for years with an unforgiving heart and not seen a single answer. Some Christians have even become cynical about the matter of prayer. "I've heard all that stuff about moving mountains before," they will say. "But it doesn't work! I've never seen God move miraculously in my life." It just may be because you have been unwilling to forgive those who have wronged you.

WE MUST FORGIVE IN ORDER TO BE FORGIVEN

Jesus made it very clear that we can only expect to be forgiven when we are willing to forgive. God cannot forgive us until we are willing to forgive others. Although He has a great flood tide of forgiveness for us, He is bound to restrain it until we ourselves forgive those who have wronged us. He is willing to forgive all our sins, mistakes, and blunders by the power of the blood of Christ, but we will never feel forgiven until we are willing to forgive.

"I just don't have it in me," someone once told me. But I reminded him that none of us has it within ourselves to forgive. Forgiveness is a gift of God. It is the result of His grace at work in our hearts. Whenever I face the forgiveness of someone who has offended me, my flesh says, "No," but my spirit says, "Yes."

All of us have that spiritual battle inside us between our carnal and spiritual nature. Whenever my flesh resists spiritual truth, God seems to say, "Richard, just think about Jesus! What would He do?" As I begin to focus my heart on Him, I remember that He was beaten, cursed, spat upon, ridiculed, and crucified. A crown of thorns was jammed onto His brow; blood ran down His face. His back was beaten raw by a cat-o'-nine-tails whip. He was stretched upon a cross and nailed to it through His feet and hands. Then He was suspended on it between heaven and earth. There He bore my sins and the sins of the whole world. Yet, as He looked down from the cross at the jeering mob that abused Him, He said, "Father, forgive them, they know not what they do."

If Jesus Christ could forgive us, how can we not forgive those who have wronged us? The real heart of the matter of forgiveness is realizing that God is greater than all our hurts. He can deal with those who wrong us if we are willing to forgive them. Who has hurt you? Is it your wife, your husband, your parents, an ex-wife, an ex-husband, a former business partner, your boss, or your friend? Whoever it may be, God can enable you to fully and completely forgive them.

Bring your hurts and your unforgiving heart to the Lord. Let God heal your hurts and mend your heart through the power of forgiveness.

*And the Lord said unto Satan, Hast thou
considered my servant Job, that there is
none like him in the earth, a perfect and
upright man, one that feareth God,
and escheweth evil? Then Satan
answered the Lord, and said, Doth Job
fear God for nought? But put forth thine
hand now, and touch all that he hath,
and he will curse thee to thy face.*

JOB 1:8, 9, 11

10

How to Keep On
Keeping On

The study of Job is one of the most incredible accounts
in Scripture. It is set in the days of the ancient patri-
archs, and it revolves around the experiences of a
wealthy herdsman named Job. It also reveals the cosmic spiritual struggle that goes on in heaven behind
the scenes of this life.

As Job is introduced in the Bible book that bears his
name, we are told that Job was a man of great wealth
and substance. He had 7 sons and 3 daughters, and he
was blessed with 7,000 sheep, 3,000 camels, 500 yoke
of oxen, and 500 donkeys. By today's standards, Job
would have been a Rockefeller or a Getty. He would

have driven a Rolls Royce and lived in a mansion. He was wealthy beyond normal comprehension.

The Scripture also tells us that he was a righteous man who loved God, goodness, and his family. The King James text says that he "eschewed" evil, meaning that he despised it with all his heart. The Bible also emphasizes that Job's wealth was a blessing from God. Job was certainly a man blessed of God and one who used his wealth to bring glory to God.

But in the cosmic realm of heaven, we read that Satan appeared before God and complained that Job only served Him because God had so abundantly blessed him. Then, Satan challenged God to come against Job and predicted that if He did, Job would turn against Him. Instead, God told Satan, "Behold, all that he hath is in thy power; only upon himself put not forth thine hand" (Job 1:12).

God emphasized a great spiritual truth, and that is that Satan has no power over our lives except by the permission of God. So in time, Satan took all of Job's possessions. Wealth could easily be lost in the ancient East, and so it was with Job. In one day bandits stole all his sheep and cattle. His herds were devastated and his servants slaughtered. Then, before the day was over, a desert storm collapsed the house where his children were, and they were all killed.

Devastated by these personal tragedies, Job simply responded, "Naked came I out of my mother's womb, and naked shall I return thither: the Lord gave, and the Lord hath taken away; blessed be the name of the Lord" (Job 1:21). The Scripture further explains that in all that happened, Job did not sin against God with his heart.

Again God pointed to Job as an example of personal integrity to Satan, but this time the Devil argued that if He could touch his body with illness, Job would turn against God. "Skin for skin," Satan said, "yea, all that a man hath will he give for his life. But put forth thine hand now, and touch his bone and his flesh, and he will curse thee to thy face" (Job 2:4–5). But again God refused to touch His servant. "Behold, he is in thine hand; but save his life" (v. 6).

This time Satan struck down Job with a terrible disease. Job came down with boils which covered his entire body from head to foot. Job had not only lost what he loved most—his children—and what he valued most—his possessions, but now he lost his health as well.

As the scene opens in this section of the story, Job is sitting in a pile of ashes, pathetically scrapping himself with a broken piece of pottery. He has been reduced to the trash pile of life. Can you imagine his suffering and pain? Broken and rejected, he sits there all alone. Now even his wife and friends could not understand his agony.

His wife cried out in frustration for Job, to just curse God, and die (Job 2:9). "Why don't you just get it over with?" is what she would have said in our terminology. "Why fight it? It's not worth it!"

But Job replied, "Shall we receive good at the hand of God, and shall we not receive evil?" (v. 10). Eventually, even Job's three friends who had come to console him, ended up accusing him of hiding some secret sin. Their consolation turned to condemnation and criticism. Just when he thought things could not possibly get worse, they did. Now his wife and friends had given up on him.

But in all this, Job did not let his faith in God waiver. In spite of his personal pain, he learned to keep on keeping on by the grace of God. And because of that faith, eventually God vindicated him and blessed him with ten more children and twice as many possessions as he had before. Job knew that he could depend on God no matter what went wrong. We too can learn how to handle life's toughest problems as we come to the realization that when all goes wrong, God is going right. He is still moving on our behalf with our greatest good as His greatest interest.

The real question for each of us to ask ourselves is, How are *we* doing with our problems? Has Satan ever bombarded you and gotten you down? Has he ever pulled the rug out from under your life and left you in a heap of ashes? If he has, this is no time to quit. We all get down at times. When we do get down, we get lonely and start to wallow in self-pity, feeling like nobody understands our pains and our problems.

Whenever we get down, we tend to think that we are the only ones suffering in all the world. We feel like nobody understands or nobody really cares. That is when Satan comes along and says, "Hey, nobody really loves you anyway. You're worthless. You've blown it! Why don't you just give up? You're a nobody!"

Whenever the Devil tries to beat you down like that, remember Job. In spite of all his troubles and even the rejection of his wife and friends, Job hung in there with God. He put his confidence in God's personal integrity and trusted Him with his very existence.

HANG ONTO THE PROMISES OF GOD

Job's greatest source of strength was this: He believed in the promises of God. He knew in the depth of his heart that he could trust God to be true to what He had promised and bring him through his troubles. There is absolutely nothing that can occur in our lives that God has not promised to see us through.

In Psalm 121:1–2, we read, "I will lift up mine eyes unto the hills, from whence cometh my help. My help cometh from the Lord, which made heaven and earth." This makes it clear that God will be there to help us when we cannot help ourselves. He is mighty on our behalf. In the same passage we read, "He will not suffer thy foot to be moved: he that keepeth thee will not slumber" (v. 3). Just think of the fact that God never sleeps as He watches over us and no trouble that comes our way can catch Him off guard! Once we accept Christ as our Savior, God is with us, ready to love and help us in our time of need. We have His promise on that!

In Proverbs 18:10, the Bible tells us, "The name of the Lord is a strong tower: the righteous runneth into it, and is safe." God is our refuge in times of trouble. He may not always choose to keep us *from* trouble, but He has promised to keep us *through* our trouble. There is not one difficulty or perplexity of life that God cannot help us overcome. He has promised to be our refuge from all the storms of life.

There are many examples from nature used in the Bible to illustrate God's protection for our lives. One is that of an eagle who watches over her brood and protects them under her wings during times of storm. As the rains fall and the winds blow upon that nest, the mother eagle keeps her eaglets protected by her wings. In the same manner, when the storms of life bombard us, God covers us with His protection and tells us to rest in His promises.

One of the great examples of faith in the Bible was Abraham, who believed the promises of God. The Lord called him to leave his native city of Ur in ancient Babylon and travel to that outpost of civilization called Canaan. So Abraham believed the promises of God, picked up his wife and their belongings, and headed for Canaan.

Abraham had no friends to welcome him into this strange new place, but he had the confidence that God went with him. And in spite of his personal struggle over the promise that he would have a son and that his seed would possess the land, Abraham persevered by faith in God's promises. Romans 4:18 explains, "Who against hope believed in hope." In other words, when all human hope was gone, Abraham hoped on in the Lord. He kept on keeping on because he believed the promise of God.

RELY ON THE PROVISION OF GOD

A promise is only as good as the one who makes it. Behind every promise is a promisor who must make good his promise. The Bible tells us that God Himself is the great provider who brings His promises to fruition in our lives.

Our hope is not just in the promises of God but in the Person of God Himself. He is the One who stands behind His promises. There is an old Black spiritual which says, "He's got the whole world in his hands." And indeed He does. God is the creator and sustainer of life. He is the One who spoke the world into existence. He made us; He sustains us; and He keeps us in the palm of His hand. He is also the same One who said, "I will never leave thee, nor forsake thee" (Hebrews 13:5).

Job was able to endure life's calamities because he had a Provider who was greater than His provisions—God Himself! Job was not trusting in his riches; he was trusting in his God. He was not relying on his friends to see him through; he was relying on the provision of his God to meet his needs.

True faith will face any disaster with the confidence that God will see us through it. The Bible promises us, "Eye hath not seen, nor ear heard, neither have entered into the heart of man, the things which God hath prepared for them that love him" (1 Corinthians 2:9).

God knows exactly *what* we need and *when* we need it. He is the great Provider of all our needs, but He wants us to learn to trust Him to make provision for us. It is one thing to know that God can provide, but it is another thing to know that He will provide exactly what we need when we need it.

When I was a child, my father told me a story that taught me to persevere through life's difficulties. He told me the story of two frogs that were hopping through a barn where a farmer was milking a cow. When the farmer finished, he got up to care for one of the animals and left the bucket of milk sitting on the floor of the barn.

The two frogs came upon the bucket and wondered what was inside. One suggested that the other one hop into the bucket to investigate.

"I'm not going alone," he replied.

"Very well," responded the other frog, "I'll jump in if you will."

Well, they both took a big leap and landed in the milk. At first, they were splashing around having a big time until they realized they couldn't get out of the pail. Then, as they began to tire from swimming around, the one frog looked at the other and said, "We might as well give up. We're never going to get out of here!"

"Oh no," said the other frog. "We can't give up now. We have to keep on trying."

"Not me," said the first frog. "I've had enough. I'm going to give up!" Bloop . . . bloop . . . gloop! Down he went into the milk and drowned.

The other frog kept splashing and kicking, splashing and kicking, until finally, to his amazement, the milk began to clabber, and after a while it became a plug of butter. Then the frog hopped on top of that plug of butter and jumped out of the bucket.

My father looked at me and said, "Son, there may be times when you feel like you're drowning. You may even want to give up altogether. If you do, down you will go. Remember, son, a child of God never gives up. He keeps on kicking because he knows God is in control. And God will always make a way out for those who trust Him and never give up!"

REALIZE THE PRICE HAS
ALREADY BEEN PAID

We can learn to endure the problems of life because the price that is necessary for our deliverance has already been paid. God knew that we could never save ourselves. He also knew that we could never pay for our redemption. Therefore, God paid the price for us. You see, becoming a Christian is a free offer of God's grace, but the cost of our salvation isn't cheap. It cost God the sacrifice of His dear Son who died for our sins that we might be set free.

In a very real sense, God paid for our salvation. I believe it is time we realized what Jesus did for us. The prophet Isaiah said, "He was wounded for our transgressions, he was bruised for our iniquities" (Isaiah 53:5). Jesus paid a price more precious than gold or jewels. He gave Himself for our salvation.

It took me several years of preaching to come to a full realization of what Christ did for me. I knew about His physical suffering. I knew that He was beaten with a whip until His back was ripped open like raw flesh. I knew that He was bruised beyond recognition and nailed to a cross. I knew that He bled and died on the cross. I even knew that He looked down on the angry mob with eyes filled with compassion.

But it took a work of the Holy Spirit in my heart to fully comprehend that Christ did all of that for *me*. He suffered for my sins. He died for every wrong thing I will ever do upon this earth. Not only did He die for me, but for every man, woman, or child who has ever lived.

When we try to envision Jesus on the cross, we tend to see only His *physical* suffering. But the greatest agony that day was His *spiritual* pain. As Jesus hung on the cross, God poured out our sin upon Him. Jesus took our place and suffered on our behalf. As God the Father looked down from heaven, He saw Jesus as a condemned sinner and poured out all of His divine wrath upon that sin.

In that moment God saw your sin and my sin and judged it once and for all time. Our sin was put to death in Jesus Christ. When He died on the cross, He took your place, bore your sin, and received God's judgment against that sin. He went through all of that for you because He loved you.

In that moment of condemnation and separation, Jesus cried, "My God, my God, why hast thou forsaken me?" It was for you and for me that He endured such punishment. But He finally triumphed over our sin and cried victoriously, "It is finished!" In that moment our redemption was sealed.

I don't know about you, but I will never give up because I don't want my Savior to have died in vain. He paid for my redemption, and I'm not going to let Satan rob me of the joy of my salvation. I'm not going to let him discourage or defeat me because my Lord went through too much for me. He died that I might live.

KEEP YOUR EYES ON THE PRIZE

The Bible is filled with accounts of human beings who kept on by keeping their eyes on their ultimate destination. They were able to persevere because they never lost sight of the goal. The Apostle Paul said, "I press toward the prize of the high calling of Jesus." You and I have a destiny with Christ in heaven. We are not just living for ourselves or the pleasures of this life, but we are living with heaven in view.

Job understood that his ultimate destiny was not the ashes or even the grave. Despite all his troubles, he said, "For I know that my redeemer liveth, and that he shall stand at the latter day upon the earth. And though after my skin worms destroy this body, yet in my flesh shall I see God" (Job 19:25–26).

Job never lost sight of the prize of eternal life. After all he had suffered, he was still convinced that God was alive, that he belonged to Him, and that one day God would resurrect his mortal body to stand again upon the earth. That is what real faith is all about. It is the personal belief that we are destined for the resurrection. Whatever goes wrong here will be corrected there.

It was that faith in the prize of God's provision that kept Job going during his toughest hours. And it is that same kind of faith that you and I need to face our most difficult trials as well. You may feel a lot like Job. You may be broken, devastated, and deserted, but God has not forsaken you. He is going to deliver you. Even when family and friends reject us, God's love still accepts us just as we are so that He can make us into what we ought to be.

If God loved you enough to send His Son to die for your sins, He loves you enough to get you through your problems and troubles. Don't give up! The price has been paid, and the prize awaits.

I leave you with these final words from Job. The testimony of one who had seen the fires of trouble and kept on keeping on. He said, "Thou shalt forget thy misery, and remember it as waters that pass away" (Job 11:16).

11

Jesus Cares for You

Not long ago I received a telephone call from a woman in her mid-thirties who had recently been divorced. She was sobbing on the other end of the phone as she tried to tell me of the heartbreaking things she was going through. Her husband had left her for another woman. After the divorce, her teenage daughter had run away from home.

This young mother proceeded to tell me how she had searched all over America looking for her daughter. She spent hundreds of dollars on telephone calls and finally located her daughter in a distant city. She bought an airplane ticket at great expense and flew to the city to bring her daughter home. When she finally found her daughter, the mother threw her arms around her, told her she loved her, and asked her to come home.

Bitter from the pain of her parents' divorce, the girl pushed her mother away. "I don't love you or Dad," she snapped harshly. "And I never want to see you again. Get out of my life and leave me alone."

Her mother was weeping as she recounted this story to me over the phone. "Pastor, I don't know if I can go on," she sobbed. "Nobody loves me; nobody wants me; nobody cares what happens to me now."

It may be that you are reading this today and you feel very much like she felt. Perhaps you feel that nobody loves or cares about you. If so, I want to share with you what I shared with that young mother that day. I believe with all my heart that Jesus loves you and cares about you more than you could ever know. No matter what mistakes you have made or what kind of mess you may be in, He still loves you.

The love of Christ is beyond measure. It cannot be compared to degrees of human love. To illustrate His compassion for us, Jesus compared His love to that of a shepherd who would leave ninety-nine sheep in the fold and risk all to search for one that was lost. In the Parable of the Lost Sheep (Luke 15:3–7), Jesus told of the seeking shepherd who pursued a single sheep until he rescued it and carried it home on his shoulders rejoicing.

Paralleling the story of the lost sheep to that of lost humanity, Jesus said, "I say unto you, that likewise joy shall be in heaven over one sinner that repenteth, more than over ninety and nine just persons, which need no repentance" (v. 7). What a beautiful picture our Lord painted with His words. In this great analogy He expressed how much He cares for us.

HE KNOWS US INDIVIDUALLY

I have often wondered how a shepherd could know that one specific sheep was missing from the fold. There is no indication in the story that he had to be told the sheep was missing. No undershepherd announced it to him. Rather, our Lord indicated that the shepherd knew each sheep individually; therefore, he knew which one was missing. He didn't have to keep a running count to know one was missing. He knew *which* one was missing.

By using this analogy, Jesus reminds us that He knows each one of us individually. You are not just a number in the mind of God; you are a specific person of individual significance to the Lord. That fact helps us to understand that God cares about us individually and personally. Although Christ came to save the masses of humanity and die for the whole world, He also came to die for you individually and specifically. And regardless of all our problems, mistakes, and errors, God loves us individually and personally. He knows your name and your needs, and He is prepared to meet the deepest longings of your heart.

I once read a story of a census taker who knocked on the door of a home. When the woman of the house answered the door, the census taker asked her a series of questions. Finally, he asked, "What is the number of your children?" The woman thought for a moment and said, "I don't understand what you mean." The census taker replied, "I need to know the number of your children."

"You must be mistaken," the woman responded. "Sir, my children don't have numbers; they have names!"

That is how God treats His children. He calls us all by name. You will never read in the Bible that God called somebody, "Hey, you." He always called people by their names—Adam, Abraham, Jacob, Moses, Samuel, and Mary. God knows us individually. The Bible tells us that He even knows the number of the hairs on our head.

Becoming a Christian is also an individual matter. You are not a Christian just because your parents are Christians. God doesn't have any grandchildren. He accepts us one by one. The fact that your father or mother may be Christians is irrelevant to the matter of whether you are a true believer yourself.

All too often people think they are Christians because they attend a certain church or belong to a particular denomination. Jesus Himself made it clear that not all who called Him Lord were truly saved (see Matthew 7:21–23). He even went so far as to tell Nicodemus, a ruler of the Jews, that he must be born again (John 3). Our Lord did not commend the ruler's righteous life and urge him to continue on with his good works. Rather, Jesus made it clear to him that his works could not save him apart from spiritual rebirth.

Just as Christ knows us individually, so we must know Him individually and personally. He is not just a religious symbol. He is a real person who can be known in an intimate and personal way. I remember once hearing a little girl saying the Lord's Prayer incorrectly. She got the words wrong, but she got the idea right when she said, "Our Father which art in heaven, how does He know my name?"

No matter how impersonal the modern world may seem to be, God is still a personal God seeking us on an individual basis and calling us to abide under His care.

HE SEEKS US PERSONALLY

I have always been impressed by the simple fact that the shepherd in the parable went seeking the lost sheep personally. He didn't send an assistant or delegate the responsibility to a committee. He went himself to find the sheep. He didn't even send another shepherd to try it first. He went himself.

Whenever I try to comprehend the simple truth that Christ left heaven for me personally, I am absolutely astounded. Why would the King of Creation leave His throne and be born in a manger to pursue one of His creatures? What advantage was it to Him? Why should He leave the glory of heaven to risk all on the cross for me? Yet the greatest fact of history is that Jesus Christ did exactly that. He who had dominion over all powers subjugated Himself to human flesh. He could have sent an angel, but He came in person that starry Bethlehem night to claim us for Himself.

Someone has said, concerning that night . . .

> That night when in the Judean skies
> The mystic star dispensed its light,
> A blind man moved in his sleep—
> And dreamed that he had sight!

That night when shepherds heard the song
Of hosts angelic choiring near;
A deaf man stirred in slumber's spell—
And dreamed that he could hear!

That night when in the cattle stall
Slept child and mother cheek by jowl,
A cripple turned his twisted limbs—
And dreamed that he was whole!

That night when o'er the newborn babe
The tender Mary rose to lean,
A loathesome leper smiled in sleep—
And dreamed that he was clean!

That night when to the mother's heart
The little King was held secure,
A harlot slept a happy sleep—
And dreamed that she was pure!

That night when in the manger lay
The sanctified who came to save,
A man moved in the sleep of death—
And dreamed there was no grave.

Author Unknown

No one else could have accomplished our redemption. Only the sinless Son of God could lay down His life as an acceptable sacrifice for our sins. Only His blood could wash away our iniquity and set us free from the penalty of condemnation we deserved.

In your moments of greatest doubt or personal struggle, you might question whether or not God really loves you. When you find yourself struggling like that, remind yourself that God loved you so much that He sent His Son to die for you personally. Whenever a person lays down his life for someone else, he has done all he could do to prove his love for that person.

When I think of those who gave their lives in Vietnam, Korea, or during World War II, I am amazed at their love and devotion. They gave all they had that we might be free. In a very real sense, they gave their lives for us. Yet some have questioned their integrity and commitment, especially those who fought in Vietnam. I find that hard to understand. Whenever someone lays down his life for others, he or she has given the ultimate measure of their devotion.

By the same token, how can anyone question the love of Christ? How can we dare suggest that He does not care for us when He gave His life for us on the cross? He did not die as a martyr or a victim. He died willingly and deliberately in our place. He was not murdered; He laid down His life intentionally. He was not caught in an inescapable series of events. He came into this world to die for our sins and then to triumph over them by His resurrection. The crowd may have called for His crucifixion. The governor may have permitted it. The priests may have demanded it, but Jesus Christ laid down His own life deliberately on our behalf.

HE CARRIES OUR BURDENS

In our Lord's parable about the lost sheep, we notice that the shepherd tenderly picked up the sheep and carried it upon his shoulders. He could have reprimanded it and ordered it home, but he picked it up and carried it home instead.

We have a little brown poodle at home named Ginger. Little Ginger is like a member of our family. She even has her own room in our basement. When we come home and open the door of her room, she comes bounding out excitedly jumping all over us. We pick her up and hug her because she is a dear little friend.

It is often said that a dog is a man's best friend. She can't talk back to us. She has never made an ugly remark or an unkind comment to us. She is just a source of unconditional acceptance and joy to all of our family.

I can imagine the joy of that little sheep when he was found by the shepherd. I can picture him, lost, alone, cold, and afraid. I can see him struggling to stay afoot on the craggy mountain ledges. I can see the panic in his eyes as he hears the distant howling wolves.

The strange thing about sheep is that when they get lost, they become helpless and cannot find their way. They must be sought, or they could be forever lost. In the beauty of our Lord's parable, the shepherd went searching for the sheep and called it to himself.

Jesus said that sheep only respond to the voice of their shepherd who calls them all by name (John 10:3). "The sheep follow him," our Lord explained, "for they know his voice" (John 10:4). He then announced, "I am the good shepherd: the good shepherd giveth his life for the sheep" (John 10:11). He also explained that He knows His sheep, calls His sheep, and gives His life for His sheep. "My sheep hear my voice, and I know them, and they follow me: and I give unto them eternal life; and they shall never perish, neither shall any man pluck them out of my hand," Jesus further explained (John 10:27–28).

Can't you just picture this helpless little lost sheep? Suddenly, he hears the shepherd's voice. "That's my shepherd," he thinks. Animals do think, you know. Then he bleats out his cry for help. The shepherd hears that little bleat and comes and takes the little sheep in his arms. The shepherd holds him close and calms his fears and then hoists him onto his shoulders and carries him home.

Our Lord could not have chosen a more appropriate picture to illustrate His love for us. How more vividly could He tell us to trust Him to carry our burdens and bring us safely to heaven? "I will take you just as you are," is what He is implying by this parable. "I will love you and forgive you." Then He puts us on His shoulders and carries us home.

HE KEEPS US SAFE

In the Parable of the Lost Sheep, Jesus said that the shepherd took him *home* to the fold. God does not find us in order to lose us. He does not forgive us and then condemn us. As we have already seen, He gives us *eternal* life. The unique quality of that spiritual life is that it lasts forever. It is not eternal one moment and then temporal the next. It lasts forever, and those who have it live forever.

When Christ claims us for Himself, He brings us into a permanent and eternal relationship with Himself. Once He puts you on His shoulder, He will never let you down. Once you are safe within His fold, you will never be lost again. God's love is unconditional. It is based upon His grace and not our merits. His is not a conditional love that demands that we meet His criteria in order to remain in His fold.

If our security depended on our ability not to fail, we would all be lost. Our security depends upon His power to save us and to sustain us. We can persevere because His Spirit is at work in us.

The gospel, in a nutshell, is stated in John 3:16, "For God so loved the world, that he gave his only begotten Son, that whosoever believeth in him should not perish, but have everlasting life." *Everlasting* is a powerful word. The dictionary describes it as that which remains for all time. The biblical term is synonymous with the word *eternal*. In other words, the salvation which Christ offers us is that which places us safely, securely, and permanently in heaven forever.

This salvation is God's free gift to mankind. He offers it willingly and freely to all who will repent and take it by faith. That is why Jesus said there is joy in heaven "over one sinner that repenteth" (Luke 15:7). Nine hundred sixty-nine times the Bible calls us to repent. It is the message of the prophets, of John the Baptist, of Jesus, and of the apostles.

Repent means to "change your mind" (Greek, *metanoeo*) in the New Testament and to "turn" or "change your direction" (Hebrew, *shub*) in the Old Testament. Thus, the full biblical picture of repentance is a change of mind about one's sin which results in a change of direction in one's life.

Christ, our Shepherd, has left the fold of heaven to seek us among the rocks of this life. When He finds us, He saves us because we cannot save ourselves. He rescues us from destruction and carries us home to heaven.

When we forsake all human effort to save ourselves and cast ourselves on His mercy, we will always find Him ready to receive us. It doesn't matter how badly you may have failed, He has succeeded in securing your redemption. It doesn't matter what you may have done wrong, He has done right for you. It doesn't matter who has rejected you, He will accept you for He is the gentle Shepherd who cares for you!

*And the Lord turned, and looked upon
Peter. And Peter remembered the word
of the Lord, how he had said unto him,
Before the cock crow, thou shalt deny
me thrice. And Peter went out, and
wept bitterly.*

LUKE 22:61–62

12

Help for Those
Who Have Failed God

It was at the last supper that Peter made his pledge of
allegiance to Jesus. He promised to defend Him unto
the death. But no sooner had he spoken these words,
when our Lord told him that he would deny Him three
times before the next morning.

Before the night ended, Jesus and His disciples
left the upper room and made their way to the Garden of Gethsemane. There they were encountered by
Judas and a band of Roman soldiers. Judas betrayed
the Lord into their hands, and Jesus was arrested and
led away captive. In the panic that followed, all the
disciples fled for their lives. Only Peter and John

WHEN THE HEART IS HURTING

made their way to the high priest's palace to witness the trial.

It was there in the courtyard of the high priest's estate that Peter was recognized three times by those who had seen him with Jesus. Each time Peter denied their accusations and refused to be identified with his Master. Thus, in a few moments, while the illegitimate trial was proceeding during the night, Peter denied Christ three times just as the Lord had predicted.

Have you ever failed God? Have you ever promised to serve Him and then turned right around and fallen flat on your face? Perhaps you were in trouble and promised God something in desperation. "I'll serve you, Lord," you may have said. "I'll do whatever you want me to do."

But when the moment of testing came, you failed the Lord. Perhaps you made your promise of allegiance when you were at a spiritual high in your life. You may have been excited about what God was doing in your life at that moment. Perhaps you had high expectations for the future.

Sometimes we get so excited about our walk with God that we forget that it is only by His grace that we can persevere. We start promising to do things that we cannot humanly fulfill. When the pressures of life come upon us, we come into temptation. When the opportunity to take our stand for Christ arrives, we often blow it altogether. There are very few Christians, if any, who have not failed God somewhere along life's journey.

And always when we do fail, there is a great temptation to give up. Satan loves to tell us how worthless we are and beat us down with guilt and defeat. But when all seems hopeless, God always reminds us that there is still hope.

REASONS FOR FAILURE

The story of Peter's denial reveals several reasons why we fail in our walk with God. As we study these reasons, examine your own life. Ask yourself, "Am I failing in any of these same areas?" Let God examine your heart, your motives, and your actions. Remember, a few steps in the wrong direction can lead to disaster.

1. He Followed Afar Off.

The first reason for Peter's failure was his refusal to remain identified with Christ. After the betrayal and arrest, the Bible says, "And Peter followed afar off" (Luke 22:54). To be sure, Peter at least tried to follow the Lord to see what would happen next. But he made sure that he kept his distance. He didn't want to get too close to Jesus now because it might cost him something.

It is impossible to successfully follow Christ at a safe distance. Either you are with Him or you are not. Ironically, millions of Americans claim to believe in Jesus Christ, but they do not want their Christianity to cost them anything. The problem is that we cannot follow Him at a distance without losing sight of who He is and what His claims are on our lives.

Jesus Himself put it this way, "No [man] can serve two masters: for either he will hate the one, and love the other; or else he will hold to the one, and despise the other" (Luke 16:13). We cannot follow Jesus and the world at the same time. They are opposing forces pulling us in opposite directions. It is a human impossibility to live for Christ and live for the desires of the flesh.

The Gallup Polls tell us that millions of Americans claim to have had an experience with Christ and that millions more desire to know more about Him. But while He was here on this earth, Jesus said that if one wanted to be His disciple, he must deny himself. Christ said, "If any man will come after me, let him deny himself, and take up his cross daily, and follow me" (Luke 9:23). The word "deny" means to "disown" or "put to death" in the Greek text. In other words, the true follower of Christ does more than give intellectual assent to Him. The true Christian must be willing to crucify himself, his desires, and his plans and surrender himself to the will and purpose of God.

Those who want to follow Christ from afar today are those who give lip service to Him on Sunday but who follow the world the rest of the week. They claim to believe in Him, but they do not want that belief to cost them anything. These are "Sunday morning Christians," and that is all! Some are only Christmas and Easter Christians and no more!

No wonder they are failing in their walk with God. No wonder there is no spiritual power in their life. No wonder their children do not respect their religious beliefs. No wonder they are not growing spiritually either. You cannot win in the Christian life by keeping your commitment at a distance. Peter's first step toward failure was that he followed afar off. Peter tried, but Peter denied.

2. He Followed the Wrong Crowd.

When Peter arrived at the palace of the high priest, he entered the gate and went into the courtyard. The trial was taking place on the balcony of the palace, and everyone in the courtyard below had a clear view of the proceedings.

The Bible says, "And when they had kindled a fire in the midst of the hall (the courtyard), and were set down together, Peter sat down among them" (Luke 22:55). In the parallel accounts in the other gospels, we read, "and Peter stood with them and warmed himself" (John 18:18), and that he later "sat with the servants, to see the end" (Matthew 26:58).

Peter's second great mistake was that he got in with the wrong crowd. These were not the fellow disciples who could encourage him to be faithful in his walk with God. These were the servants of the priests who were determined to put Jesus to death. Peter found himself mingling with those who hated and despised Jesus. They were the keepers of the temple and the servants of the palace.

As incredible as it seems, Peter stood by the enemies' fire, warming his hands and then sat down among them as though he thought he could get lost in the crowd. Here was Christ's disciple sitting with the Christ-haters who were determined to destroy everything Peter claimed to believe.

Whenever you think you can just blend into the crowd, you are seriously mistaken. Yet, many professing Christians are doing today what Peter did then. They are trying to be part of the world without denying Christ. It didn't work then, and it won't work now. Peter was there hardly any time when people began to question whether or not he was one of Jesus' disciples. The reason Peter denied Him was that he had already put himself in a position of compromise which led to failure.

The old-timers used to have a saying: "Lay down with the dogs and you will get up with the fleas." How right they were! Any time we hang around with the wrong crowd, we are bound to start doing the wrong things. Remember Peter's initial boldness and confidence? He was the disciple who wasn't going to fail, but he did because he got in with the wrong crowd.

As Peter sat there with the servants, he could see Jesus being accused and condemned by those who had brought Him to the high priest. He could see them mocking Jesus, hitting Him, and spitting on Him. I am sure that a sense of panic must have gripped him as he watched this ordeal. There was no way he wanted to be identified with Christ in that setting, but it wasn't long until the servants began identifying him. They knew he was different. They even sensed that he didn't belong there because he wasn't one of them.

If you want to overcome failure, you will need to take a strong and clear stand for Christ. Let people know what you believe right up front. Stay away from those who would drag you down into defeat. Peter was strong, or so he thought, until he got in with the wrong crowd.

3. He Failed to Obey God's Word.

Peter ignored the warning of Jesus. He didn't fall into sin out of sheer ignorance. Jesus had warned him about his over-confidence at the last supper earlier that evening. "Satan hath desired to have you, that he may sift you as wheat," Jesus had warned Peter (Luke 22:31).

But it is evident that Peter never took Jesus' warning seriously. Perhaps you have been like that. You have heard the warnings of Scripture time and time again, but somehow you have thought they didn't apply to you. They have gone in one ear and out the other. If we won't listen to God, we cannot hope to succeed in our spiritual lives.

Peter ignored all that Jesus tried to tell him. He didn't even take any basic precautions. He walked right into the courtyard and sat down with the enemy! But it wasn't long until they began to question his relationship to Christ. You may try to hide your Christianity from others, but you will always stick out like a sore thumb. The real tragedy is that these servants asked Peter to identify himself and he couldn't do it. He not only failed Christ, but he also failed to be a witness to these servants.

The three denials came quickly, one upon the other. Before he ever realized what he was doing, Peter had denied his Lord three times in succession. Think of it! Here was Jesus' best disciple deliberately denying that he ever knew Him. No sooner had the words of denial fallen from his lips than the rooster crowed and Peter's heart sank within him.

Have you ever fallen like that? In a moment of weakness or pressure, you virtually denied Christ in your life. Have you ever lied about your relationship to Him? Have you ever given into temptation in a moment of weakness? Have you failed in some area of your life and questioned whether God could ever use you again? If you have, then you know that sinking feeling. That feeling of denying your faith in Him.

REQUIREMENTS FOR RESTORATION

But the wonderful thing about God is that He never leaves us without hope. Even when we have failed Him, He will never fail us. When it seems the bottom has fallen out of your life, God's mighty hand will uphold you and bring you back.

Failure is never an easy process. It is humiliating and heartbreaking. It hurts both us and others. It is certainly not something to be desired, but when it happens, it need not be the end of all hope.

There are four requirements for forgiveness and restoration given in the story of Peter's denial. They are all stated within two verses of Scripture where the Bible says, "And the Lord turned, and looked upon Peter. And Peter remembered the word of the Lord, how he had said unto him, Before the cock crow, thou shalt deny me thrice. And Peter went out, and wept bitterly" (Luke 22:61–62).

1. He Realized Christ Was Watching.

The great turning point came in Peter's life when Jesus turned away from His accusers and looked at Peter, who had just denied Him for the third time. Twice Peter had insisted that he did not know Jesus, and finally he shouted out his third denial above the noise of the crowd. The rooster crowed, and when Peter looked up, Jesus was looking right at him.

As Peter looked into Jesus' eyes, his heart was broken. He could see the love, the hurt, and the disappointment of His Savior looking back at him. Peter broke because he realized he could not escape the Savior's gaze. The Bible reminds us that "the eyes of the Lord run to and fro throughout the whole earth" (2 Chronicles 16:9).

Wherever you go and whatever you do, you can be sure that God is watching. He knows our deepest thoughts and our most hidden secrets. Those things that you can hide from others cannot be hidden from God. Every time you sneak into some questionable place or get involved in some questionable practice, God is there and sees what you are doing. You cannot escape Him.

2. He Remembered Jesus' Words.

As soon as Peter realized Jesus was looking right at him, he remembered what He had said. Unfortunately, we often have to come to the end of the line or the bottom of the barrel before we remember God's warnings. There is just something about human nature that causes us to forget God's truth when all is going well. We start thinking that we can make it on our own.

When the bottom falls out of our lives, we usually realize that what God said was true all along. Only then are we usually willing to face up to the truth. But let me remind you that every warning, every principle, every truth in Scripture is given to us for our own good. Each one of those truths was given by a God who loved us and cared about our deepest needs. Despite all our mistakes and failures, He remains a God of compassion who loves, forgives, and restores us to useful service to Him.

3. He Removed Himself from the Place of Temptation.

The Bible says that Peter "went out." It means exactly what it says. He left the comfort of the fire and the crowd of servants and went out into the night alone. As he did, he removed himself from the place of temptation and defeat.

Some people make the mistake of thinking that they are strong enough to handle temptation. They go into places where they are vulnerable to sin. They let down their guard under the excuse that what they do is their own business. But what we do is God's business because we are His children.

If you really want to overcome temptation, you must be willing to remove the source of that temptation. I read a story many years ago about a man named Trochilus, a friend of Plato, the great philosopher. Trochilus loved the sea, and he loved to go sailing any time he could. But he loved it so much that he often took risks, and one day he nearly lost his life in a shipwreck. Later he vowed that he would never sail again.

When Trochilus returned home, he stood at his window looking out to the sea that had nearly taken his life. Then he called in a brick mason and had him wall in the window and brick it over so that he could not see the view. Then he explained to Plato that he had the window walled up because he was afraid that a morning would come when he might look out the window at the beautiful sea and be tempted to sail again. That's the kind of action that many of us need to take in dealing with temptation as well—to wall up the windows of our hearts!

4. He Came to Genuine Repentance.

Peter was so broken by the sin that he had committed, that he rushed out and "wept bitterly." His tears were tears of repentance. They were evidence of godly sorrow and a broken spirit. His pride was shattered, and in remorse he wept over the wrong he had done.

Tears alone are not necessarily proof of repentance. One might cry and never change. In Peter's case, his tears were evidence of a true heart that was broken, and his changed life became a testimony to all who knew him. In fact, when most of us think of Peter, we think of his great exploits, not his great failure.

His life stands as a ray of hope to everyone who has ever failed God. Here was a man who failed in the worst way possible. He violently denied that he ever knew Christ. Yet, afterwards he was forgiven and restored to service by the Lord Himself (see John 21).

On the Day of Pentecost, recorded in Acts 2, Peter, the apostle who had once denied Christ, stood and boldly spoke of his faith in the risen Christ. Time and time again, he risked his life to preach the gospel and thousands were converted under his preaching.

If you have failed the Lord, there is still hope for you. Though your heart may be broken and your spirit crushed, God can mend your broken heart, revive your spirit, and renew your service. The key to restoration is repentance. Turn away from your sin, and turn to Christ.

Part Four

BLESSED ARE THE PURE IN HEART

Blessed are the pure in heart: for they shall see God.

Matthew 5:8

13

Why We Do the Things We Do

Have you ever asked yourself why you do the things you do? I've asked myself that question many times. Perhaps you have come under conviction about some habit or behavior in your life, and you determined not to do it again. The Holy Spirit seemed to convict your heart and revealed some area of sin in your lifestyle.

"All right, God," you said, "I know what I've done is wrong, and I promise I won't commit that sin again." With renewed determination you faced Monday morning with a real sense of victory. You even made it through Tuesday, Wednesday, and Thursday. But by Friday you found yourself yielding to temptation again. Frustrated and discouraged you asked yourself, "Why am I doing this?"

If that is your question, you are not the first one who has asked it. Ever since the Garden of Eden, people have been asking this question. Even the great Apostle Paul struggled with this question. And in Romans 7, Paul wrestles with the question in his own heart. To paraphrase his remarks, he says, "It seems to be a fact of life that when I want to do what is right, I inevitably do what is wrong. I love to do God's will so far as my new nature is concerned, but there is something else deep within my lower nature that is at war with my mind and wins the fight. It makes me a slave to the sin that is still within me. In my mind, I want to be God's willing servant, but instead I find myself enslaved to sin. My new life tells me to do right, but the old nature that is still inside me loves to sin. Oh, what a terrible predicament I'm in. Who will free me from my slavery to the deadly lower nature? Thank God, it has been done by Jesus Christ our Lord" (Romans 7:19–25, TLB).

Like all of us, Paul struggled with the conflict between the spiritual and the physical urges of life. But he learned how to handle the struggle successfully, and so can you and I.

THE WAR WITHIN

In order to win the war between the spirit and the flesh, we need to understand the nature of the conflict. It is a spiritual struggle for the control of our lives.

1. The Nature of the Flesh.

The sin nature that we were all born with is our fleshly nature. It is our nature to sin. Ephesians 2:3 says we are "by nature the children of wrath." Romans 3:23 tells us, "For all have sinned and come short of the glory of God." This does not mean that everyone has committed every sin possible, but it does mean that the totality of our being has been corrupted by sin.

Some may object to this teaching, saying that they were not born with a sin nature. But if we were not born with such a nature, who taught us to sin? Did someone teach us to rebel against our parents, throw temper tantrums, or insist on having our own way? Did someone teach us to become jealous, hateful, angry, or vindictive? No, we discovered it on our own. Our behavior was disgusting because *we* were disgusting. It was part of our nature to be that way. All of us were born with sin in our lives. No matter how hard we try to make that old sinful nature better, we cannot improve upon it.

The prophet Jeremiah said, "The heart is deceitful above all things, and desperately wicked: who can know it?" (Jeremiah 17:9). The word "desperately" means *incurably*. The prophet's conclusion about human nature is that our hearts are so sinful that we are incurably wicked beyond our own comprehension.

Even our best and kindest deeds cannot eradicate our sinful nature. You can attend church, give money to the poor and needy, sing in the choir, get baptized, and go through all the motions of religion and still fall short of God's demand for righteousness and holiness. Apart from His divine intervention in our lives, the best things we can do are "filthy rags" in His sight.

2. The Nature of the Spirit.

The Bible tells us that God has a wonderful solution to all our problems. That solution is described as a "new heart" or a "new birth." When it occurs, a marvelous thing happens within us. The prophet Ezekiel explains it like this, "A new heart also will I give you, and a new spirit will I put within you" (Ezekiel 36:26). This incredible promise is one of a *new* nature.

Throughout your life you have been controlled by the old nature of sin, but now God promises to give us a new nature. Day in and day out, the only nature you have ever known was that old sinful, fleshly nature of self, but now God tells us that we can have a new nature of the Spirit.

One day my heart was convicted by the Holy Spirit that I was a sinner. I came to realize that I was personally responsible for my sin. I also realized that I could not change my sinful nature and that I could in no way save myself. But just as I was convicted of my sin, I was also convinced that Jesus Christ died for my sins and made my salvation possible. I repented of my sin and by faith turned to Christ to save me. I believed that His death was the sufficient payment for my sins. What I experienced was a new birth in Christ. It was a spiritual rebirth that theologians call *regeneration*.

It was the issue of the new birth that was the central topic of Jesus' discussion with Nicodemus, a Jewish religious leader, the main character of our discussion in chapter two. Our Lord told Nicodemus that he needed the regenerating work of the Holy Spirit within his heart. He said, "Except a man be born again, he cannot see the kingdom of God" (John 3:3). When Nicodemus questioned how one could reenter his mother's womb,

Christ explained that He was speaking of a spiritual birth (John 3:5).

In discussing this issue, Jesus made it clear that which is "born of the flesh is flesh" and that which is "born of the Spirit is spirit" (John 3:6). The nature of the flesh cannot of itself produce the nature of the Spirit. Only the Spirit of God can do that within our hearts. This is the great news of the Bible. God does for us what we cannot do for ourselves. He gives us His Spirit and regenerates our old fleshly hearts with a brand new nature.

3. The Nature of the Conflict.

Spiritual conversion results from regeneration by the Holy Spirit, but it doesn't eradicate the fleshly nature within us. The fleshly (carnal or sinful) nature did not merely dissipate. It is still a reality that must be dealt with properly. Otherwise, we would become sinlessly perfect after we were saved. Now some people may believe that and some preachers may even preach that, but I have never met a sinlessly perfect person. We all make mistakes, and we all still sin. We may not be able to sin without coming under conviction, but believers are still capable of sinning because we still struggle between the nature of the flesh and the nature of the Spirit.

Let me clarify the nature of this conflict. The Holy Spirit dwells in us at the point of conversion or salvation. He produces a new nature within us, but He does not eradicate our old nature of sin. Therefore, it is inevitable that there will be a conflict between these two natures within us. Thus, the battle between the Spirit and the flesh erupts. The Spirit says, "Do the things of God." But the flesh says, "No, do the things of the flesh."

The Apostle Paul describes this inner struggle in Galatians 5:17, where he writes, "The flesh lusteth against the Spirit, and the Spirit against the flesh." He further describes these two natures as "contrary the one to the other." They are never in agreement with each other. Therefore, we often find ourselves being tempted to do the very things we really don't want to do.

No matter how long you may have been a truly committed Christian, you will find at times a war going on within you. The most prominent time this is demonstrated is in the hour of temptation. The flesh says one thing, and the Spirit says another thing. The flesh says, "Yield," but the Spirit says, "Stand your ground."

The Bible is filled with accounts of God's people who battled with the struggle over temptation. Joseph was frequently enticed by his master Potipher's wife while serving as a slave in their home (Genesis 39). The Bible tells us this situation went on "day by day" (v. 10). Yet, Joseph determined to stand his ground against her and refused to sin against God.

On the one hand, the flesh may well have said, "Go ahead, Joseph. She is a beautiful woman. She's lonely and begging for your attention. No one will ever know." But on the other hand, the Spirit may well have said, "Don't do it, Joseph. You know better than that. You are God's chosen servant. Flee away from her."

Finally, Joseph fled from the house rather than sin against God. Even though she falsely accused him, Joseph retained his integrity.

But the Bible also tells us about David, who lusted

after Bathsheba. Again, the flesh said, "Take her. You deserve someone like her." But the Spirit said, "Don't touch her. You are God's anointed servant." David turned a deaf ear to the Spirit and yielded to temptation. Soon one complication led to another, and David's life became filled with deception and even murder. Though he later repented, he lived to regret his actions for the rest of his days.

Life is a series of choices. You and I are free moral agents who must choose to obey the Spirit or the flesh. From the time you get up in the morning until you go to bed at night, your life is filled with many choices. Whatever choices you make will determine the outcome of your life. You must choose between the Spirit and the flesh.

WINNING THE BATTLE

"I understand that there is a spiritual battle going on within me," a young man recently admitted to me. "But what can I do about it? How can I win this battle?" he seemed to plead.

I am convinced that God did not save us and give us a new nature so that we might be frustrated and defeated. I am convinced that He can empower us to overcome sin and the flesh by the power of His Spirit.

1. Recognize Temptation for What It Is.

Temptation is a plot, a scheme, or trick of Satan. It is designed to sidetrack your spiritual growth and to ruin your life. Satan is the master of camouflage. He can make sin alluring to the flesh. Even though he is fallen from heaven, Satan has the radiance of color and music in his bones. He can use every means at his disposal in this world to trick us into sinning. He makes it look so good, so enticing, so desirable. He never shows us its ultimate consequences.

Sin may look glamorous for a moment, but there is always a disastrous hook in every temptation. It may appeal to our eyes, our flesh, or our pride, but it will inevitably destroy us. If you are ever going to win the battle with temptation, you must recognize it for what it is—a trick of Satan to destroy your life.

2. *Realize the Contamination of Sin.*

Sin is like a poison. It is the great contaminator of life. It pollutes every aspect of our being and spreads faster than the common cold. Sin is the rotten apple of the soul. You know that old saying that one rotten apple can spoil the whole barrel of apples. Sin is like that rotten apple, polluting all that it touches.

Sin cannot be easily contained. That is why we can't tolerate a little sin in our lives and assume it will not affect the other areas of our lives. It's like having a tiny scorpion in your bed. It may be small, but its sting is great, and sooner or later it will get you.

3. *Remember the Consequences of Sin.*

The Bible warns us that "the wages of sin is death" (Romans 6:23). Throughout the pages of Scripture we are warned that one day we will have to pay the consequences of our sin. Sin stalks us like a lion stalking its prey. One action leads to another. Every choice results in a consequence, and soon our lives can become a tangled complication because of sin.

"I'm not going to worry about that," you may say. "I'll just go ahead and sin and then confess it, and God will forgive me."

Unfortunately, there are a lot of people who use that excuse, but it won't work! While God is a forgiving God who delights in forgiving our sins, He only forgives that which comes from a repentant heart. The attitude that says, "I can keep sinning and keep repenting" is not the expression of a truly repentant heart. First, a genuinely repentant person will not keep on deliberately sinning. Second, every sin has spiritual, emotional, and physical consequences that are not always eliminated by confession and repentance. If you keep on sowing sin, you are going to reap its disastrous consequences in your life.

As a pastor, I hear tragic story after tragic story of those whose lives have been wrecked by sin. Even when they have accepted God's forgiveness for their sins, they carry its consequences in their consciences, in their souls, in their hearts. If you want to win the battle with temptation, focus on the serious consequences of sin and don't give in to it.

4. *Rely on the Holy Spirit for Strength.*

Despite the daily struggle we all have with the flesh, the Bible assures us: "Greater is he that is in you, than he that is in the world" (1 John 4:4). Victory over temptation comes when we rely on God's grace and not our own self-effort. We cannot win the conflict by ourselves; we must have His help.

The Bible also tells us, "There hath no temptation taken you but such is common to man: but God is faithful, who will not suffer you to be tempted above that ye are able; but will with the temptation also make a way to escape, that ye may be able to bear it" (1 Corinthians 10:13). Three things stand out in this promise. First, your struggle is not unique to you. It is common to all of us. Take hope; you're not alone in the battle. Second, God will limit the temptation so that it is possible for you to resist by the power of the Spirit. Third, there is always a "way of escape" if you will take it.

Spiritual warfare is a normal part of the Christian life. But the promise of God is that He will empower us to overcome the world, the flesh, and the Devil by the power of His Spirit. The Scripture promises, "Walk in the Spirit, and ye shall not fulfil the lust of the flesh" (Galatians 5:16).

If you want to win the battle within, recognize temptation for what it really is—a *trick*. Realize the extent of its contamination—*total*. Remember its consequences—*trouble*. Finally, rely upon the Holy Spirit for the *triumph!*

What shall we say then? Shall
we continue in sin, that grace may
abound? God forbid. How shall we, that
are dead to sin, live any longer therein?

ROMANS 6:1–2

14

Can a Christian Continually Sin?

Can a person who claims to be born again continually
live in sin and still be true Christian? That is a question
that is being debated by many today and has been for
centuries. Out of that debate believers have been di-
vided, churches have been split, and religious denomi-
nations have been formed.

On one end of the extreme are those who believe
that because they still have the potential for sin,
through the fleshly nature that remains in them, they
are destined to sin almost daily, continually falling
away from God and coming back to Him through forgiveness. On the other end of the extreme are those

who believe that they can live in sinless perfection here on earth, never making the mistake of committing sin, always pure and perfect.

But almost needless to say, there are many who are caught between the two extremes in their search for a holy lifestyle. They realize that they are not perfected yet in holiness, but there is also something terribly wrong with the idea that a true believer can continually live in sin. And, indeed there is! Well, the debate can go on endlessly, but the bottom line of the matter is this: *What difference is salvation making in the way we live?* The answer to that personal question is by far the most important.

Almost daily we read about heavy metal rock stars, extortionists, gamblers, homosexuals and x-rated movie queens who claim to be "born-again Christians." Is that really possible? Can a Christian deliberately and willfully sin against everything he or she claims to believe?

It may be that you are reading this today and asking yourself if your salvation experience made any difference in the way you lived. Perhaps you still struggle with the same problems, temptations, and desires as you did before you claimed to be saved.

In Romans 6, the Apostle Paul deals with this same issue. Having emphasized the greatness of God's grace and His willingness to forgive our sins, Paul asks the question, "Should we continue in sin then that grace may abound in our lives?" His answer is, "God forbid" (v. 2), or to put it another way, "absolutely not." Our forefathers said it like this: "two wrongs don't make a right." Another way of expressing it is, "It's never right to do wrong in order to get a chance to do right." In other words, you don't rob a bank to get money to give to the church.

A RIGHT UNDERSTANDING OF SIN

Once we understand the seriousness of sin, we won't likely be so quick to excuse it. The Bible tells us that the unbeliever is blinded to the issue of sin. He cannot understand its consequences nor comprehend its seriousness. Paul explains that "the god of this world hath blinded the minds of them which believe not" (2 Corinthians 4:4). Therefore, we have a better understanding of why lost people often indulge themselves in sin—they don't know any better.

But when a professing Christian claims that he is going to deliberately and willfully sin against the very God he thinks has saved him, that is astounding. For a Christian to live in deliberate sin is violating the very things he or she claims to believe. Such behavior contradicts the very nature of salvation itself. Yes, a Christian is certainly capable of sinning, but he will also certainly come under conviction for that sin until he repents of it and turns away from it. A right understanding of sin and its consequences certainly verifies this truth.

First, *sin makes us its slave*. In addressing the issue of sin in the believer's life, Paul said, "Let not sin therefore reign in your mortal body, that ye should obey it in the lusts thereof" (Romans 6:12). Whenever we let sin dominate our behavior, it rules our spirit and controls our body. When sin reigns in your life, you become its servant. Then you don't just have the sin, the sin has you!

Ask anyone who has ever become addicted to alcohol, drugs, or pornography if it enslaves. They will tell you horrible stories of the vice-like grip that sin has on their lives. Why can't the alcoholic or drug addict quit? Because sin enslaves!

The person who is addicted to sexual perversion is equally enslaved. Many broken-hearted men and women have admitted to me that they wanted to stop but could not seem to overcome their addiction. "I just can't control myself," they often say. What they are really saying is that sin has control of their lives.

Most of us have read about the trial, conviction and execution of mass murderer, Ted Bundy. He was convicted of murdering two young girls, but was also suspected of murdering at least thirty-eight other college coeds. When asked why he did it and why he didn't stop, I remember hearing it reported that Bundy's only answer was, "I just couldn't help myself."

Ted Bundy became the slave of sin, but his addiction was like that of any person addicted to sin. Once it has its grip on your life, you are its slave. You may tell yourself that you could quit if you really wanted to, but if you really wanted to quit, you would quit.

Second, *sin leads to shame.* There is nothing beautiful about sin. It eventually leads us to shame and contempt. When David sinned against God in committing adultery with Bathsheba, he wrote, "My bones waxed old through my roaring all the day long. For day and night thy hand was heavy upon me" (Psalm 32:3–4).

David's sin led to depression and shame that resulted

in physical, as well as spiritual, consequences. When a true believer sins, he is overcome with shame. He will not long attempt to excuse or justify his sin. He cannot because he knows it is wrong. The shame that comes into our lives is the result of the convicting power of the Holy Spirit who indwells us. He will not let us keep on sinning and get away with it.

I would certainly question the genuineness of anyone's salvation who claimed that he could deliberately and continually live in sin without coming under spiritual conviction. The Bible clearly tells us that the Spirit of God convicts us of sin, righteousness, and judgment (John 16:8–11). When a person claims to be righteous but keeps on sinning, he is really admitting that God is absent in his life.

Third, *sin results in spiritual separation.* The Bible emphasizes the holiness of God. It makes it clear that we cannot even approach God by ourselves because He is so holy that men literally fall dead before Him. Our only hope of fellowship with God is through the righteousness we receive by faith in Jesus Christ. He alone makes us acceptable to God, but that does not mean that we who have been saved can just live any way we choose.

The Bible also asks, "What fellowship hath righteousness with unrighteousness?" (2 Corinthians 6:14). The two are mutually exclusive of one another. God is holy and righteous, and He does not tolerate sin. Whenever we let sin dominate our lives, we are rejecting God's rightful place of authority and control over us.

The prophet Isaiah warned the sinful Israelites, "Your iniquities have separated between you and your

God, and your sins have hid his face from you" (Isaiah 59:2). Whenever we live in deliberate sin, God hides His face from us. Yet, one of the most pitiful things in the world is a believer who deliberately sins against God but who does not realize what is happening in his (or her) life. This person inevitably loses the joy and security of his salvation. Not only that, but he also loses his sense of direction and ends up confused and defeated.

Believers who got into sin always ended up in trouble in the Bible. Think of Samson, who could conquer the Philistines but could not conquer his own passions. He became involved in a sexual affair with Delilah that eventually cost him his hair as well as his life. After his fateful haircut, the Scripture tells us that he went out to fight his enemy as at other times and did not realize that "the Lord was departed from him" (Judges 16:20).

You can't live in sin and expect the power and blessing of God to be upon your life. Once a believer sins, he places himself in a position of separation from fellowship with God.

Fourth, *sin always leads to suffering.* Sin is never an end in itself. It always leads to disastrous consequences. The Bible warns: "when lust hath conceived, it bringeth forth sin: and sin, when it is finished, bringeth forth death" (James 1:15). The Apostle Paul put it this way: "the wages of sin is death" (Romans 6:23). History is littered with the wrecked lives of those who thought they could sin against God and get away with it.

Sin is not something with which to trifle. It has more than just spiritual dimensions. Sin has psychological, social and physical dimensions as well. Even when we are forgiven by God spiritually, there may be other consequences to our sin that are long lasting. For example, you may get drunk and fall through a plateglass window, severing your arm. You can be forgiven, but you won't get your arm back.

Often those who have given themselves over to habitual sins truly repent and receive God's forgiveness, but it takes years for people to forgive them. Such sin damages one's testimony and credibility. It may take many years to rebuild it. Perhaps the greatest tragedy of all is when people cannot forgive themselves for their sin. They know intellectually that forgiveness is available to them, but they keep themselves in psychological torment because of past sins.

There is a story of a young boy who visited his grandfather one summer on the old family farm. Not being used to the rules of the farm, the boy soon got into trouble. Day after day, it was one mischievous deed after another. Finally his grandfather decided to teach him a lesson by making him pound a nail into the barn door every time he did something wrong. It didn't take long before the barn door was filled with nails. By the middle of summer, there was no room to put any more nails in the old door.

Then grandfather explained to the boy that every time he did something good, he could go, take the claw hammer and pull one of the nails out. He became so excited that all he seemed to do was good, and time after time, after every good deed, grandfather let him pull out another nail. Why, by the end of the summer every nail was gone but one.

One day the little fellow had done a good deed and

came to his grandfather and said, "Granddaddy, I've only got one nail left, come on and watch me pull it out!"

"All right," Granddad said, "Let's go do it!"

Excitedly, the little boy put the claws of the hammer around that nail and pulled. Suddenly it popped out of the door and hit the ground. He picked it up, ran to his grandfather and said, "Look, Granddaddy, the last nail, now I've undone all I did wrong."

But the wise old grandfather then turned the boy's face to the barn and said, "Son, the nails may be gone, but look at the scars you left on the barn door!"

How true a lesson for all of us. We can repent our sins and be forgiven, but sin may leave scars behind that will cause things never to be the same.

A RIGHT UNDERSTANDING
OF SALVATION

When a person claims to be saved or born again, what are they really saying about themselves? What is true Christianity? What does it mean to be converted to Christ? When we claim that He is living within us, what are we really saying about ourselves? The Apostle Paul explained it like this when he wrote, "our old man is crucified with him . . . that henceforth we should not serve sin" (Romans 6:6). I believe that Paul was emphasizing the importance of a total commitment of ourselves to God resulting in the spiritual transformation of our lives.

The apostle goes on to explain that we should walk in "newness of life" because of our spiritual rebirth.

Thus, salvation results in a brand new life in Christ. In a similar passage, Paul says, "Therefore if any man be in Christ, he is a new creature: old things are passed away; behold, all things are become new (2 Corinthians 5:17).

1. Salvation Changes Our Destiny.

When you accept Jesus Christ as your personal Savior, your destiny is changed from hell to heaven. You are no longer headed in the same direction. The goal has been radically changed. When Christ became your Savior, He paid the penalty for your sins, removed the condemnation of hell, and put you on the road to heaven.

2. Salvation Changes Our Disposition.

Once the spirit of God enters our lives at conversion, He begins to change our outlook and attitude on life itself. No longer are we viewing the world around us from the vantage point of unbelief. Now we begin to see spiritual truth for the first time.

Once you become a child of God, you are no longer comfortable with the things of Satan. You may occasionally go back to the old ways of sin, but you won't stay there. You can't stay there because it is not your nature to stay there.

If a sheep were to fall into a mud puddle, what would he do? He would push, strain, and struggle until he got out of the mud. Why? Because it is not the nature of a sheep to want to stay stuck in the mud. But if a pig were to wander into that same mud puddle, he would wallow in it for hours because it is his nature to do so.

The same contrast is true between a believer and a nonbeliever. The believer may fall into the mud of sin, but he is not going to want to stay there and wallow in it because it is no longer his nature to do so. The new nature convicts him to get out of the mud. But the unbeliever can wallow in sin for years. It doesn't bother him because he doesn't have a spiritual nature.

3. Salvation Changes Our Dominion.

The Apostle Paul not only expressed the problem, but he also offered the solution. "Being then made free from sin," he wrote, "ye became the servants of righteousness" (Romans 6:18). We are set free from the dominion of sin and are made citizens of the kingdom of righteousness. We have exchanged the bondage of sin for the freedom that is in Jesus Christ.

A true Christian may fall into temporary sin, but there is no excuse for his living a life of continual and deliberate sin. To do so is to deny the faith, and in reality to admit that one has never experienced a true relationship with Jesus Christ and indwelling of the Holy Spirit.

We are all familiar with the famous Bowie knife of the frontiersman, Jim Bowie. Although the knife is well known, the story attributed to its creation is not. Yet, it is interesting, indeed. Supposedly, Jim Bowie went to visit his friend, James Black, a blacksmith, to arrange for a special knife to be fashioned for him. As Black listened to Bowie's description of the knife he wanted, one of perfect balance, and an indestructible blade, it seemed to be an impossible task. Nevertheless, the blacksmith said he would do what he could for his friend.

Several months passed and Bowie returned to the blacksmith's shop. He was handed the knife he had ordered. It was perfect in its balance. He tossed it from hand to hand, then threw it across the shop and it stuck in the blacksmith's wall and quivered. Mr. Bowie turned to Mr. Black and asked, "Blackie, how in the world did you do it? Where did you find such a substance as this?"

The blacksmith said, "One night this summer, I was looking up at the stars when I saw something streak across the sky and fall near my shop. I ran out and picked it up and put it on my shelf. When you asked for such a special knife, I remembered this rock from heaven. So I took some simple ore from the earth and melted it with that from the sky, and from this I fashioned the knife."

What was the secret? The substance from the heavens had purified and perfected the ore from the earth! Likewise, our Lord Jesus, heaven's light, came and shed His blood that all who believe upon Him might be freed from the dominion of sin, purified and separated from a world of sin and the things of it. With that in mind, listen once again to the words of the Apostle Paul. "What shall we say then? Shall we continue in sin that grace may abound? God forbid. How shall we that are dead to sin, live any longer therein?" (Romans 6:1-2).

Wash me thoroughly from mine iniquity,
and cleanse me from my sin. . . .
Create in me a clean heart, O God;
and renew a right spirit within me.

PSALM 51:2, 10

15

Confession: Keeping the Closets Clean

When I was a little boy, like most other kids, I often tried to hide it when I did something wrong. Around the house when something got broken it was usually my fault, and I would stick it in the back of the closet or under the bed. I remember breaking the keys on the piano one day—now that was a tough one! But, whenever my mother discovered it, she would get the kids together, look us dead in the eye and ask, "All right, which one of you did it?"

My brother and two sisters always had one answer, "Richard did it!"

I heard my name used that way so many times that I

thought my name was Richard "Did It" Lee. The problem was, they were usually right; Richard did do it!
Whenever I knew that I had done wrong, I would always struggle with whether or not I was going to tell
my parents or try to cover it up.

But covering up sin is not limited to the behavior of
children. One of the great issues in the hearts of many
adults is also whether to cover or confess their sins.
Psalm 51 is the prayer of confession that King David of
Israel prayed after trying to hide his sin of adultery
with Bathsheba. He had stayed behind in the palace
while his soldiers went off to war. There he saw the
beautiful Bathsheba and became involved with her
though she was the wife of Uriah. She became preg-
nant, and David tried to hide the pregnancy by having
her husband, Uriah, killed and then marrying her.

For several months his life became embroiled in
a series of lies and schemes to cover up what he had
done. But no matter how clever his attempts to hide it,
that sin hounded him day and night. He couldn't get it
out of his mind or his heart. "My sin is ever before me,"
he later admitted (Psalm 51:3).

Perhaps as you read this today, there is some sin that
has hounded you for many years of your life. Instead of
dealing with it in confession and repentance, you have
merely tried to sweep it under the rug of your conscience, but it still lies there rotting in the depth of
your soul. Every time you pick up a Bible or walk into
church, it seems that sin is brought to mind again. At
times you may feel it is more than you can bear.

David was in that situation. He had not only sinned,
but he had gone to great lengths to cover it. He went
against his own beliefs as one sin led to another. Yet,

despite all his efforts to cover his sin, he was still in bondage to it. Only when he was confronted by God's prophet did he finally repent and deal with it.

It is easy to criticize David. We might ask, "How could a spiritual leader do such a terrible thing?" But we must remember that David was a human being subject to human faults and passions like anyone else. While we never want to excuse our failures, the real issue is what we are willing to do when we fail. That moment of crisis usually reveals whether or not we really have a heart for God.

Most of us struggle with the issue of confession. We know that God promises to forgive our sins if we will confess them, and we are still tempted to lie about them and hide them. How many times have you thought, "I ought to confess this, but I'm just going to hide it."

Why is confession so hard for us? Because confession involves a declaration. It means making a statement about ourselves. It is a humbling process to admit, "I have sinned. I am guilty. I did it." There is just something about saying that that knocks the pride out of us and takes the wind out of our sails.

Confession also involves repentance. It is an admission of sorrow for sin as well as an acknowledgment of it. In the New Testament, the Greek word for confess combines two words, meaning "to say the same thing." In other words, when we truly confess our sins, we must be willing to say the same thing about them that God says. We must call it what it really is—an offense to God Himself.

Confession is the key that unlocks the heart and frees the soul. It opens our inner being to God's forgiving grace and sets us free from the sin that so easily binds our conscience. It involves admitting that we have a sin nature in general, and it also involves confessing individual sins specifically.

SIN INVOLVES A PRICE

We are more likely to confess our sin when we remind ourselves of its costly consequences. Sin is not something trivial that we can just skip over and go on as though it doesn't matter. Sin demands a price to be paid. That is why the Bible warns us, "the wages of sin is death" (Romans 6:23). If we are to guard our hearts, we must remember the high price of low living.

Remember, *sin is destined to be revealed.* No matter how clever you may be at covering it, sin will always come to the surface. You may be able to hide it from your wife or your husband. You may hide it from your pastor or your friends. You may even think you have hidden it from God, but you have not.

Jesus said, "For there is nothing covered that it shall not be revealed; neither hid that it shall not be known" (Luke 12:2). Nothing that is done in secret shall escape the judgment of God. Our Lord went on to explain that even that which is spoken in secret shall be "proclaimed upon the housetops" (Luke 12:3). The Bible reminds us that there is coming a day when all things (good and evil) will be revealed. All men shall be judged by the standard of God's righteousness. We will have to give an account of every word, every deed, and every action in our lives.

In the Book of Revelation, we are told that the books of God will be opened at the judgment and every sin in our lives will be listed there. Every one that has not been confessed will be listed against us. That day of judgment will be a terrible day for those who are not prepared to meet God.

Our sins will not only be revealed before all at the Judgment, most of them will be found out in this life as well. Numbers 32:23 tells us, ". . . and be sure your sin will find you out." Notice the Bible did not say that your sin would be *found out*, but that your sin would *find you out*. You see there is something about sin that makes it want to come out from its hiding place in the shadows of the heart and shout aloud its existence.

In recent years we have seen political figures, religious leaders and men and women of great renown having their sins broadcast on the nightly news and blasted across the headlines of our newspapers. Most of them were caught in foolish, compromising situations that to the thinking man or woman simply shouldn't be. Many have asked, "How could these people be so foolish? So blatant? So poor in their judgment?" Well, the answer is that sin has its own way of making certain it's found out. In fact, the Scripture said that you can be *sure* your sin will be revealed.

But for those who repent of their sins, the moment they stand before Christ will be one of rejoicing. The Bible urges us, "Repent ye therefore, and be converted, that your sins may be blotted out, when the times of refreshing shall come from the presence of the Lord" (Acts 3:19). Our greatest hope for the day of judgment will be that we have already confessed our sins and they have been blotted out before God.

Remember, *sin demands cleansing*. In David's prayer of confession, he prayed, "Wash me thoroughly from my iniquity, and cleanse me from my sin" (Psalm 51:2). He realized that his soul was dirty and needed to be cleansed. Like David, many of us need to take the soap of confession, with the brush of repentance, and ask God to scrub us with the water of forgiveness so that we might be made clean.

Unfortunately, we often try to convince ourselves that we don't really need such cleansing. I have traveled through the villages on the mission field and watched as the natives came out to meet us in their finest attire; they thought they had done their best, but by our standards they were still filthy dirty. Many of us are like that in our spiritual lives. We think we have done our best, but we fall far short of God's standard of righteousness.

Many of us need to take the standard of God's Word and examine ourselves in light of its truths. We need to stop kidding ourselves and face up to things the way they really are in our lives. The Bible warns us that many will profess faith in Christ—and even claim to have done wonderful works in His name—but they will be turned away in the Day of Judgment (see Matthew 7:21–23) because they have never turned away from their sins.

Perhaps you have never really turned to Christ by faith in Him. You have never experienced His cleansing power in your life. Until now you may have seen no need for repentance. Could I remind you that you really do need Him. You desperately need His forgiveness and cleansing, and it comes by trusting His shed blood and His death on the cross as sufficient payment for your sins.

Unfortunately, there are some Christians, and you may be among them, who were initially cleansed, who have been living in sin for so long that their consciences have been seared or dulled to its seriousness. The Holy Spirit initially convicted you, but you have resisted His conviction for so long that you barely feel Him tug at your heart anymore. Let me urge you not to turn a deaf ear to the voice of conviction in your soul. Let God take control of your life again and the joy of your salvation will spring up anew within you.

All sin must be cleansed. We cannot hope to enter heaven without the application of Christ's cleansing blood to our sinful hearts. We must confess our individual sins in order to keep our fellowship fresh and vibrant with God.

GOD IS THE ANSWER

The most important person in our life is God Himself. He is the key to all other relationships. Whenever we have sinned against someone, we need to realize that we have ultimately sinned against God. It is His standard that we have violated, and it is with Him that we need to make the offense right.

1. God's Position Is Holiness.

Sin is that behavior which falls short of God's standard. It involves our "missing the mark" of His righteousness. That is why God is justified in judging sin. He is a holy God who cannot and will not tolerate sin.

In David's prayer of confession, he acknowledged, "Against thee, thee only, have I sinned, and done this evil in thy sight: that thou mightest be justified when thou speakest, and be clear when thou judgest" (Psalm 51:4). He too realized that God was just in condemning his sin. He knew that God would not tolerate such behavior because of His holiness.

When the Scripture asks the question, "What fellowship hath righteousness with unrighteousness?" its implied answer is, "None!" Why? Because God has no fellowship with that which is unrighteousness. Whenever we sin against His holiness, we remove ourselves from fellowship with Him. We don't lose our salvation, but we certainly lose its benefits and blessings.

2. God's Pleasure Is Forgiveness.

The amazing thing about God is that He not only judges sin but He delights in forgiving sin. He never leaves us hopelessly beyond the reach of His grace. In fact, He delights to do for us what we cannot do for ourselves. He loves to forgive repentant sinners who confess their sins to Him. It is no wonder that the converted slave trader, John Newton, wrote the hymn, "Amazing Grace," in response to his own conversion. There surely is something amazing about a God who can love us enough to forgive us.

In response to his own confession, David said, "Then will I teach transgressors thy ways; and sinners shall be converted unto thee" (Psalm 51:13). David realized that all he had been through had taught him the depth and greatness of God's forgiveness. He also realized that he was now in a position to teach that kind of forgiveness to others.

God not only judges sin, but he forgives it. What a wonderful and glorious hope for every person who is willing to acknowledge that truth. It is the realization that His greatest pleasure comes in forgiving our sin.

3. God's Power Is Victory.

God not only forgives our sin, but He also gives us victory over sin. The Bible says, "For we are his workmanship, created in Christ Jesus unto good works, which God hath before ordained that we should walk in them" (Ephesians 2:10). Think of it! You are the artistic creation of God's grace. Your spiritual life is the product of His work in your soul. He has created spiritual life within you for His own good pleasure and your blessing. He not only saves and forgives, but He keeps on shaping us into the very image and likeness of Christ Himself.

I was walking through a shopping mall once when I noticed a beautiful sculpture display. There were several masterpieces of sculpture on a very high shelf, and as I wondered why they were placed up so high, some children walked by and started toying with one beautiful piece on a lower shelf. I then realized why the other sculptures had been so carefully positioned on the highest shelves. There were even cards placed around the displays saying, "Hands off," or "Do not touch." One card even said, "Absolutely!!! Do not touch!"

Each artist was adamant about protecting his or her workmanship. As I stared at the sculptures and their warning signs, I was reminded of the fact that we are God's workmanship and He has placed His "Hands off" sign on us. Satan cannot touch us without the permission of God. He has placed a hedge of protection around us. As long as we are in the hands of the divine potter, we are in the place of His protection.

OUR RESPONSE: CONFESSION

Once David faced the seriousness of his sin and sought the forgiveness of God, he realized the great cleansing that comes from confession. It opens the closet of the soul and releases the raging animal of guilt and sets us free. He also discovered that his confession of sin benefited others as well.

Whenever we deal with sin in our lives, God uses us to convict others to do the same. The whole nation of Israel had their eyes on David. Their response to their own sin was dependent on his response to his sin. When he repented, he took away any excuse they may have tried to offer for their sin. The influence and impact of his life was such that it taught Israel the importance of dealing with sin.

Whether you realize it or not, people are watching your life. Family, friends, colleagues, and co-workers alike may be watching how you live to see if Christianity is as real and life-changing as you claim. The influence of your life and testimony could well be the key to seeing others come to Christ as well.

Confessing our sins not only helps others, but it helps us as well. It restores us to a right relationship with God and rekindles the joy of our salvation. The

Bible promises, "If we confess our sins, he is faithful and just to forgive us our sins, and to cleanse us from all unrighteousness (1 John 1:9). This promise is so total in its scope that it means that every single sin, mistake, or error you have ever made can be forgiven and blotted out forever if you will but confess it. And that is the key to keeping the closets of our heart clean before Him.

But sanctify the Lord God in your hearts: and be ready always to give an answer to every man that asketh you a reason of the hope that is in you with meekness and fear.

1 PETER 3:15

16

A Reason for Hope

Several years ago a U.S. Navy submarine sank off the coast of Massachusetts in a terrible storm. With great haste, the Navy dispatched its finest rescue teams to the scene of the disaster. In time the divers located the ship and attempted to rescue the crew. For several hours their only means of contact with the crew trapped inside the submarine was by tapping on the hull with a metal instrument. The crew inside the submarine did the same, tapping out a message by the dots and dashes of the Morse Code. The crew inside the submarine did the same, tapping out a message by the dots and dashes of the Morse Code.

Unfortunately, as the hours passed, the rescuers were unable to upright the vessel and set the crewmen free. Finally, the rescuers lost all contact with the crew inside the submerged submarine. The tapping signal stopped, and all was silent on the ocean floor. Then in a faint and distant sounding tap, the rescuers heard a crewman's desperate message: "Is there any hope?" "Is there any hope?"

As I watched the news account, my heart was filled with sorrow for these dying men, but also I thought of the awful spiritual plight of millions of people who are just as desperately asking, "Is there any hope?"

I've heard it said that a person can live about forty days without eating food, about four days without drinking water, and about eight minutes without breathing air—but a person can't live one minute without hope!

In a world of tension and confusion where it seems society has lost all sense of direction, we need to know that there is hope for our future. We need to know that there is something real and genuine to build our lives upon as we look ahead.

It was this hope that Peter was reminding his readers of when he wrote about the "reason of the hope that is within you" (1 Peter 3:15). Peter realized that the confidence a Christian has as he faces the difficulties of this life is a hope the world does not understand. It is an inner spiritual confidence that goes beyond normal human comprehension.

The Psalmist understood that same hope when he wrote Psalm 42. Though apparently he was discouraged and defeated at the time, he also realized God had not abandoned him without hope. As he struggled with life's toughest issues—the issues of the heart—he came to grips with life-changing truths. He found the reasons for hope. We can find them, too.

GOD'S PRESENCE IS WITH US

As he searched his soul and uttered his prayer to God, the Psalmist said, "My soul thirsteth for God" (Psalms 42:2). He realized that God was the living Lord. He understood that God, not he, was the ultimate reality. Our only significance is not within ourselves, but it lies in the fact that God lives with us.

Today, more than ever, people need to know that God is alive. They don't need more religion or even more churches. What people really need is a deep and personal experience with the living God. We really don't need more statues, cornerstones, pillars, markers, churches, synagogues, or cathedrals. What we really need is a personal and spiritual encounter with the living God Himself!

As wonderful an institution as the Church is in our society, I am afraid that many of us get so caught up in our denominational affiliations that we forget all about God. I am also concerned that we often get so entangled in the redundancy of the form and ritual of religion that we miss God altogether. He is just as alive and real as you are or as your best friend or family member.

Unfortunately, most of us don't think of God in such personal terms. We tend to view Him as an abstraction, sort of floating around "out there." But God is not some vague theological or philosophical abstraction.

He is real, alive, and personal. He is not just some vague idea to be treated with irreverence and disrespect. But many people treat Him that way because they do not realize who He is.

Vance Havner, author and evangelist, tells the story of a young girl who once toured the great museums of Europe (*The Havner Notebook*, p. 224, Baker Press). Eventually, she came to a museum in Venice that housed Beethoven's piano. Intrigued by this great piano, she sat down at it and began to play some rock and roll. A caretaker heard her banging on the keys and rushed over and said, "Miss, do you know whose piano this is?"

"Yes, it's Beethoven's piano," she said.

"Then why are you playing it?" the caretaker asked.

"Oh, I like playing the piano," she said.

"Let me tell you something," he responded. "The other day, Paderewski, the great pianist, came here to see Beethoven's piano."

"What did he play?" asked the girl.

"Nothing," the caretaker explained, "Paderewski said he was not worthy to touch Beethoven's piano."

Too many of us are like this foolish girl when it comes to dealing with God. We impersonalize Him, and then we irreverently trivialize Him. We tend to become flippant about the things of God when we forget how real He is. He is not "out there" somewhere. Yes, He is the ruler of the universe. But He is also the personal and infinite God who cares about each one of us.

The greatest hope for mankind is the knowledge of God as a real, personal, and living Savior. His very presence in our lives reminds us that we are not alone as we face the future. God is on our side.

GOD'S FACE IS TOWARD US

As the Psalmist struggled in prayer in Psalm 42, he asked the searching question, "Why art thou cast down, O my soul? and why art thou disquieted in me? hope thou in God: for I shall yet praise him for the help of his countenance" (v. 5). I have often taken great hope in this passage myself. Notice the beautiful sentiment that it expresses. We can hope in God because His face is toward us. He is interested in our lives, our needs, and our problems. He is looking, gazing, and watching intently to make sure that our every need is met.

Countenance is another word for face. As we study the Psalms, we see that term used again and again. In Psalm 27:8, David said, "Thy face, Lord, will I seek." In Psalm 31:16, he prayed, "Make thy face to shine upon thy servant." What David is saying is, "God, look at me, and I know everything will be well."

In my book, *The Unfailing Promise* (Word, 1988), I told the story of a young preacher, thirty-seven years old, whose beautiful wife died from an incurable disease. As the young pastor and his little daughter left her graveside grieving and sobbing, they clung to each other all the way home. When they got home later that evening, the little girl asked if she could sleep with her father because she was afraid without her mother.

So they crawled into bed, pulled up the covers, and

turned off the light. Soon the young pastor, exhausted by the pressure of all he had endured, was fast asleep. But after a few minutes, he was awakened and startled by something he felt on his face. As he reached toward his face, he would feel the tiny fingers of his little daughter.

"What's wrong, Honey?" he asked.

"Nothing," she replied, "Daddy, I'm just feeling to see if your face is toward me."

You and I as believers can rest assured that God's face is always toward us. He loves us with a personal love that will not let us go. In our darkest and most difficult moment, He is there to assure us of His love. The God who sent His Son to die for your sins, loves you enough to keep you through your toughest times.

GOD'S STRENGTH IS WITHIN US

Every born-again child of God realizes that the Spirit of God dwells within him or her. Once He has entered our lives by faith, He takes up residence within us. God lives within the human soul of redeemed men and women.

Thus, the Psalmist prayed, "O my God, my soul is cast down within me: therefore will I remember thee" (Psalm 42:6). Despite his own discouragement, he turned his attention to God. He remembered who He was and what a difference He could make in his life. He had to remind himself of who God was and, therefore, who he was as a child of God.

Whenever we realize *who* we are and *what* we are in God, it will revolutionize the way we live. When times of discouragement or despair engulf us, we must understand that the living God is within us to empower us to do His will. We are not just imitators of God, trying to do the best we can for Him. We are the living, breathing, walking, talking children of the Almighty God.

God spoke to the Prophet Ezekiel concerning His people saying, "And I will give them one heart, and I will put a new Spirit within you; and I will take away the stony heart out of their flesh, and will give them a heart of flesh: That they may walk in my statutes, and keep mine ordinances, and do them: and they shall be my people, and I will be their God" (Ezekiel 11:19–20).

What is this new Spirit that will cause our hearts to be changed? It is the empowering Holy Spirit of Almighty God! Before our Lord Jesus went into heaven He told us of the Holy Spirit who would come. He said, "But the Comforter, which is the Holy Ghost, whom the Father will send in my name, he shall teach you all things" (John 14:26). And it is the sweet and powerful presence of His Holy Spirit that makes God's power available to us. What a promise, and what a hope! He is the source of our love, our joy, and our peace. He is the one who enables us to overcome all the trials and temptations of life. When we come to the realization of the fact that we are not alone because God's presence is not only *with* us, He is *within* us, we ought to be the most powerful and positive people on earth.

We should be like the little boy who kept pitching up a baseball and trying to hit it with his bat. He tried time and time again and missed the ball every time.

"Son, you're not much of a hitter," called out an old man watching his attempts.

"No, sir," said the little boy, "but, wow, am I ever a pitcher!"

No matter what pressures, problems, or struggles we may face in life, Christians have every reason to be positive because our lives are indwelt by the Holy Spirit, empowered of God, and destined for heaven. He is both *with* us and *in* us. He is *watching over* us and *working in* us at the same time. The living God has poured His Spirit and presence within us; therefore, we have every reason to hope. It is no wonder the Bible calls us "more than conquerors" in Christ (Romans 8:37).

GOD'S LOVING-KINDNESS
WATCHES OVER US

In Psalm 42:8, we read, "Yet the Lord will command his loving-kindness in the daytime, and in the night his song shall be with me." There is never a time, day or night, when we are not in His loving care. He always watches over us with His loving-kindness. He is always with us, and we are never left alone to struggle for ourselves without His help.

Recently I was a guest on several radio and television programs in Los Angeles. One of the stations, I was told, is the most listened-to Christian station in America. We were doing a call-in response program where listeners could call the station to ask a question of me on the air. One dear lady called in and asked,

"Dr. Lee, is it wrong for me to call upon God in my hour of need?"

The lady was so discouraged and dejected that she was even questioning whether she should call upon God for help at all. "Is He really there? Can He help me?" she asked desperately.

"Certainly," I said. "Not only is He really there, but it blesses the heart of God to answer His children in their hour of need!"

The same God, who is with us on the mountaintops of life, is also there walking beside us through the valleys. He is always the same, whether we are up or down. He is the Friend who sticks closer to us than a brother. He has promised, "I will never leave thee, nor forsake thee" (Hebrews 13:5). He also said, "Call unto me, and I will answer thee, and shew thee great and mighty things" (Jeremiah 33:3).

The invitations of Scripture are many. Time and again we hear God calling us to come to Him and lean on Him because He cares for us. In 2 Chronicles 16:9, we read, "For the eyes of the Lord run to and fro throughout the whole earth, to shew himself strong on behalf of them whose heart is perfect toward him." Notice again that God's face is toward us and His gaze is intent. He is looking for someone to bless, to love, and to give hope in their moment of despair.

Charles Wesley, brother of the famous evangelist, John Wesley, and one of the founding fathers of the Methodist Church, was walking beside a lake one day when a terrible storm arose. The wind grew fierce, the sky dark, the lightning flashed and thunder roared as the terrible storm approached. Suddenly, a frightened little bird, tossed about by the wind, flew under Wesley's coat. There it remained, shivering in fear, until the storm was over. Finally, Wesley reached in, gently taking the little bird out from its place of shelter, and released it into the calm blue sky. As he thought about the bird and its place of safety, he took his pen and wrote these familiar words:

> Jesus, lover of my soul,
> Let me to thy bosom fly
> While the nearer waters roll,
> While the tempest still is high:
> Hide me, O my Saviour, Hide
> Till the storm of life is past,
> Safe into thy haven guide,
> O receive my soul at last.

GOD'S SALVATION IS FOR US

The Psalmist ends by proclaiming God to be his "rock," Psalm 42:9, and then announces the final challenge, "Hope thou in God: for I shall yet praise Him" (v. 11). He saw that God was his only hope and yet He was also a sure foundation—a certain hope that would never fail.

There is a famous painting by G. F. Watt that is entitled "Hope." In it is the scene of a woman who has had to battle life. She is pictured as beaten and worn. She is holding a harp with all the strings broken but one. That one string is called the string of hope. Suddenly she is shown striking that one string and as she does the music of hope fills her world. In the midst of her struggle she has found the string of hope and that has made her life worth living.

For every man the music of hope is found in Jesus Christ. If someone were to ask you, "Where is your hope today?" what would you reply? Is your hope in your religion, your good deeds, your career, your health, your money? Or is your hope in the living God and the power found in His eternal salvation? The greatest issue of the heart and life is the answer to that question. God is waiting for those who will call upon Him, to be with them, to turn his face toward them, to dwell within and keep them safe in His everlasting care. Now that is a hope worth living for, and a hope that is available for all who are willing to receive it through faith in Jesus Christ.

Indeed, the many issues of the heart, which are the issues of life itself, are real and relevant to us all. So numerous are they that they could never be completely contained in the pages of this book, or any other book written by man. Although the questions of life may be many and varied, the answers to those questions all begin with a relationship with Jesus Christ as Savior and Lord. For us to know Christ is to know the very Creator of life. And who is there better to direct us along the pathway of life than its Creator? No one, of course. That is why knowing Him in an intimate and personal way is so essential. Let me invite you to receive Christ today. To accept Him personally into your life, as your Savior and Lord. As you do, you will find Him sufficient and near to guide you through many issues of the heart.